Table of Contents

- Assess third-party risks (vendors, business associates)
- Conduct periodic risk reassessments and scenario testing
- Prepare risk reports for the board and regulators

Chapter 4: Lead Incident Response Planning and Execution

- Maintain a healthcare-specific IR playbook for PHI breaches
- Define 'Code Cyber' response levels and escalation procedures
- Coordinate with clinical leads for downtime protocols
- Ensure rapid EHR access recovery is tested quarterly
- Conduct simulated phishing-based breach drills with staff
- Involve patient privacy and legal teams in breach notification
- Integrate cybersecurity into the hospital emergency management plan
- Define communication protocols for internal and external stakeholders
- Coordinate digital forensics and evidence preservation
- Conduct post-incident reviews and lessons learned exercises

---

Chapter 5: Conduct Regular Security Audits and Compliance Reviews

- Conduct internal HIPAA Security audits and policy adherence checks
- Audit clinician access logs to detect snooping or abuse
- Review remote access by contractors and medical students
- Validate system logs for EHR, PACS, and lab systems
- Align with CMS, OCR, and Joint Commission compliance frameworks
- Coordinate with internal audit or third-party compliance consultants

---

Chapter 6: Report to Executive Leadership and Hospital Board

- Provide dashboards summarizing PHI breach risks and HIPAA compliance
- Translate cyber risks into impacts on patient safety and care delivery
- Deliver incident updates tied to hospital operations
- Present ransomware readiness metrics and drills
- Report audit results and CAPA (Corrective and Preventive Actions)
- Justify cybersecurity budget tied to hospital risk posture

Chapter 7: Supervise Security Operations Center (SOC)

- Monitor for EHR anomalies, privilege escalations, and lateral movement
- Detect unusual data flows from imaging, pharmacy, and lab systems
- Correlate logs from medical devices with enterprise SIEM
- Define thresholds for alerting on hospital-specific indicators of compromise
- Conduct forensic reviews of endpoint incidents on shared nursing stations
- Ensure SOC analysts receive healthcare-specific training

Chapter 1: Develop and Maintain the Healthcare Cybersecurity Strategy

1. Align Cybersecurity with Patient Safety and Clinical Outcomes

In a hospital setting, cybersecurity is not merely an IT issue—it is fundamentally a patient safety concern. The interdependency between clinical workflows and digital systems means that any disruption to the integrity, availability, or confidentiality of information can directly impact patient care. As the CISO, aligning cybersecurity initiatives with patient safety must be a foundational component of your strategy.

To do this effectively, it is important to identify the clinical systems most critical to real-time patient outcomes—such as Electronic Health Records (EHRs), medication administration tools, infusion pumps, radiology imaging platforms, and laboratory information systems. These systems often form the backbone of patient care workflows, and even minor disruptions can lead to delayed diagnoses, incorrect treatments, or emergency room gridlocks.

This alignment also requires close collaboration with Chief Medical Officers (CMOs), Nursing Directors, and department heads. Security controls and risk mitigation strategies should be designed not only for technical robustness but also with an understanding of clinical impacts. For example, implementing multifactor authentication (MFA) should not hinder clinicians' ability to access life-saving systems in time-sensitive situations. Therefore, risk-based exceptions, context-aware authentication, or biometric solutions may be more appropriate in emergency rooms or intensive care units.

To further embed cybersecurity into clinical culture, establish KPIs that reflect both security posture and patient safety, such as "percentage of downtime for critical systems," "number of unauthorized access attempts blocked for bedside medical devices," or "phishing click rate among clinical staff." These metrics can be used to inform leadership about the tangible relationship between cybersecurity and care quality.

2. Map Strategic Priorities to Joint Commission and HIPAA Requirements

Hospital CISOs operate in a highly regulated environment. Therefore, aligning cybersecurity strategy with mandatory compliance frameworks is not just best practice—it's an operational necessity. Two primary frameworks dominate the healthcare compliance space in the United States: HIPAA (Health Insurance Portability and Accountability Act) and standards set forth by The Joint Commission (TJC).

HIPAA mandates safeguards for protecting Protected Health Information (PHI), focusing on administrative, physical, and technical controls. These include access controls, encryption, audit logs, breach notification procedures, and workforce training. The Joint Commission, on the other hand, integrates cybersecurity preparedness into its evaluations for hospital accreditation, especially under Environment of Care and Information Management standards.

To ensure full alignment, a hospital CISO should conduct a comprehensive controls mapping exercise. This involves reviewing existing policies, technical controls, and operational procedures against HIPAA Security and Privacy Rules, as well as Joint Commission requirements. Any gaps should be documented in a security strategy roadmap, with timelines for resolution and metrics for success.

In addition, many hospitals benefit from adopting and aligning with the NIST Cybersecurity Framework (CSF) or the HHS 405(d) Health Industry Cybersecurity Practices, which provide scalable guidelines for improving cyber posture while satisfying regulatory expectations.

Documentation is key. Maintain clear evidence of compliance activities such as risk assessments, business associate agreements (BAAs), and user access reviews. This documentation will serve not only during audits and surveys but also as a strategic communication tool for hospital leadership and regulatory bodies.

---

3. Conduct a Risk Assessment Focused on Patient Data, Connected Devices, and EMR Systems

Risk assessments are the foundation of any healthcare cybersecurity strategy. In a hospital, where data is constantly being created, accessed, and shared across clinical departments and third-party systems, understanding where your biggest vulnerabilities lie is crucial.

The scope of risk assessments must include:

- Patient data repositories (EHRs, data warehouses, backup archives)
- Networked medical devices (IoMT—Internet of Medical Things)
- Interfaces with third-party services (labs, telehealth, billing)
- Endpoint devices across clinical and administrative departments

Begin by cataloging all digital assets, data flows, and known vulnerabilities using tools like asset discovery systems and vulnerability scanners. Then, classify data based on its sensitivity and regulatory importance. For example, patient diagnosis codes, social security numbers, and payment information must be treated with higher scrutiny.

Use a structured framework like NIST SP 800-30 or HITRUST for conducting the risk assessment. Identify the likelihood and potential impact of various threats—ransomware attacks on EHRs, unauthorized access to PACS systems, or malware infecting insulin pumps, for instance.

After quantifying and prioritizing these risks, develop a risk register and an accompanying risk treatment plan. Mitigation strategies should balance technical feasibility, clinical impact, and regulatory requirements.

Finally, schedule periodic reassessments (e.g., quarterly or biannually), and be prepared to reassess immediately following a major incident or organizational change (e.g., system upgrades, mergers, or vendor changes).

4. Include Response Strategies for Ransomware Affecting EHR Access

Ransomware is one of the most catastrophic threats facing modern healthcare institutions. A successful attack can shut down entire hospitals, redirect ambulances, and force clinicians to revert to paper-based systems—all of which degrade patient safety and increase operational costs.

CISOs must incorporate ransomware-specific response strategies into the broader incident response and business continuity plans. This includes:

- Ensuring frequent, secure, and offline backups of the EHR and associated clinical systems
- Maintaining a tested playbook for quickly isolating infected systems and switching to manual procedures
- Defining communication plans that account for email or VoIP unavailability
- Coordinating with law enforcement and forensic specialists in case of a confirmed breach
- Training clinical and administrative staff on alternative documentation workflows during EHR downtime

EHR downtime procedures should not only be documented but rehearsed. Downtime drills are essential for ensuring that clinical staff can access critical patient information and continue safe treatment delivery when systems are unavailable.

Further, threat hunting and proactive monitoring should be employed to detect early-stage ransomware indicators such as lateral movement, privilege escalation, or unusual file access patterns.

CISOs must also weigh the legal, ethical, and operational implications of ransom payments, and ensure leadership is aligned on this front before a crisis arises.

5. Coordinate with Clinical Leaders to Align with Hospital Operations

Cybersecurity should not operate in a silo—it must be a collaborative function that engages directly with the clinicians who rely on the hospital's digital infrastructure. A successful cybersecurity strategy aligns not only with IT and compliance, but also with the unique needs of physicians, nurses, and allied health professionals.

Establish a multidisciplinary cybersecurity steering committee that includes representatives from clinical, operational, legal, and compliance functions. This group can help validate security initiatives, discuss workflow impacts, and shape future investments.

Clinician engagement is particularly vital when introducing changes that affect user experience—such as MFA, endpoint encryption, or data access restrictions. Invite frontline staff into the testing and feedback loop before rolling out such initiatives. This participatory model ensures better adoption and fewer workarounds.

Additionally, consider assigning departmental "cyber champions"—clinicians trained to serve as liaisons between the IT security team and clinical units. These champions can offer real-world insight on workflow compatibility and help cascade security awareness across their teams.

Finally, security policies and training must speak the language of clinical operations. Frame security not just as regulatory compliance but as a matter of protecting patient dignity, safety, and continuity of care.

6. Regularly Update Based on Health-Sector Threat Intelligence (e.g., H-ISAC)

In the ever-evolving landscape of cyber threats, especially in the healthcare sector, static security strategies quickly become obsolete. Hospitals face a wide spectrum of threats—from ransomware and data theft to nation-state cyber operations targeting critical infrastructure. To stay resilient, a CISO must ensure that the cybersecurity strategy is a **living document**, continuously updated with insights from real-time threat intelligence (TI), particularly health-sector-specific feeds such as **Health Information Sharing and Analysis Center (H-ISAC)**.

H-ISAC plays a critical role in aggregating, analyzing, and disseminating threat intelligence relevant to healthcare entities. It shares indicators of compromise (IOCs), alerts about ongoing campaigns (e.g., Medusa, ALPHV, LockBit), technical analysis, and remediation guidance. As a CISO, subscribing to H-ISAC feeds and integrating them into your Security Operations Center (SOC) and threat detection tools is a strategic necessity.

But raw intelligence isn't enough. The organization must also have the operational capability to **interpret, prioritize, and act** on that intelligence. This requires building an internal process for:

- Classifying TI based on its criticality and relevance to hospital assets.
- Mapping new threats to your hospital's digital and physical ecosystem.
- Correlating TI with internal logs and alerts via SIEM platforms.
- Automating detection through IOCs and behavioral analytics integration.

A best practice is to assign a dedicated **Threat Intelligence Analyst** or include this role in your SOC to maintain situational awareness and report actionable insights to the broader cybersecurity and executive teams.

Regular reviews of the threat landscape should be incorporated into **weekly SOC briefings**, **quarterly risk review meetings**, and **biannual strategy updates**. This ensures your security posture evolves in line with adversarial tactics, techniques, and procedures (TTPs).

Moreover, healthcare-specific intelligence should be shared internally with key departments. For example, if there's an uptick in phishing targeting billing departments with medical invoice lures, your finance and administrative staff should be alerted with tailored awareness campaigns.

Also consider cross-sector collaboration with regional hospitals, state/local ISACs, and public health authorities to share anonymized intelligence. Joint intelligence briefings and coordinated tabletop exercises based on current threat actors foster collective defense.

Ultimately, your cyber strategy should not be revised on an annual basis alone—it should **adapt continuously** based on the evolving threat landscape, leveraging external partnerships and intelligence sources to stay ahead of attackers.

---

7. Plan Long-Term Initiatives for Zero Trust and Endpoint Resilience

The traditional "castle-and-moat" model of hospital cybersecurity—where users and systems inside the network are trusted by default—is no longer viable. With the increase in remote work, cloud adoption, third-party access, and connected medical devices, trust must be **earned and continuously verified**. This is the essence of **Zero Trust Architecture (ZTA)**.

For hospitals, implementing Zero Trust is not a one-time project, but a **multi-year transformation** that touches identity, network, device, and application layers. As CISO, you are responsible for crafting a Zero Trust roadmap that addresses:

- **Identity verification** using multi-factor authentication (MFA), biometric checks, and dynamic access scoring.
- **Device trust** via posture assessments that ensure endpoint security (e.g., patched OS, running EDR, no malware).
- **Least privilege access** through Role-Based Access Control (RBAC) and Attribute-Based Access Control (ABAC).
- **Microsegmentation** of internal networks to prevent lateral movement between departments (e.g., separating ICU, Pharmacy, Admin).
- **Continuous monitoring** of user and device behavior through UEBA (User and Entity Behavior Analytics).

In the context of hospitals, Zero Trust must be balanced with **clinical usability**. For instance, while MFA is critical, overly aggressive enforcement in trauma wards or surgical suites could endanger lives. Therefore, risk-based authentication—triggered only for high-sensitivity actions or anomalous behavior—should be used.

Parallel to Zero Trust is the need for **endpoint resilience**. Hospitals are filled with diverse endpoints: workstations on wheels (WOWs), legacy machines running critical imaging software, mobile tablets, badge access terminals, and diagnostic devices. These endpoints often present a soft target for attackers due to outdated OSes, lack of encryption, or shared use among staff.

To ensure resilience:

- Implement **next-gen endpoint protection** (NGAV + EDR) that combines signatureless malware detection, rollback capabilities, and isolation features.
- **Segment vulnerable legacy devices** from the main network and monitor them with enhanced logging.
- Enforce **application allowlisting** and remove local admin privileges on non-clinical endpoints.
- Use **Mobile Device Management (MDM)** and **Mobile Application Management (MAM)** for phones and tablets used by clinicians.
- Regularly test endpoint hardening configurations across units, including imaging, surgery, and administration.

Also, ensure endpoint telemetry feeds into your SOC for real-time monitoring and response. Adopt **automated containment** strategies for infected or suspicious devices to prevent lateral spread before human intervention is needed.

Planning for Zero Trust and endpoint resilience is about future-proofing your organization. As hospital environments become more digital and decentralized, only a model that assumes breach, verifies every access request, and maintains endpoint integrity can sustain long-term security—and, ultimately, patient safety.

Chapter 1 Keywords and Definitions

1. **Patient Safety**
   The avoidance of unintended or unexpected harm to patients during the provision of healthcare. In cybersecurity, this involves maintaining system availability and data integrity to prevent errors in diagnosis or treatment.
2. **Clinical Outcomes**
   Measurable changes in health or quality of life resulting from healthcare services. Cybersecurity supports positive outcomes by ensuring uninterrupted access to medical records and accurate data.
3. **Healthcare Cybersecurity Strategy**
   A comprehensive plan developed by the CISO to protect clinical systems, patient data, and operational technologies from cyber threats, while aligning with healthcare regulations and mission-critical goals.
4. **HIPAA Compliance**
   Adherence to the Health Insurance Portability and Accountability Act, which mandates administrative, physical, and technical safeguards to protect the confidentiality, integrity, and availability of protected health information (PHI).
5. **Joint Commission Standards**
   Guidelines established by The Joint Commission to ensure healthcare quality and safety. These include requirements for secure electronic data management and cyber preparedness.
6. **Risk Assessment**
   A systematic process to identify, evaluate, and prioritize risks to hospital systems and data. It forms the basis for developing mitigation strategies and ensures compliance with HIPAA and other regulations.
7. **Electronic Health Records (EHR)**
   Digital systems used to collect, store, and manage patient health data. EHR systems are prime targets for cyberattacks and central to hospital cybersecurity strategies.
8. **Medical Device Security**
   The practice of protecting Internet-connected clinical devices (e.g., infusion pumps, imaging systems) from unauthorized access or tampering that could compromise patient safety.
9. **Ransomware Response**
   A structured plan to detect, isolate, and recover from ransomware attacks that lock hospital systems or data, often involving offline backups, downtime protocols, and legal coordination.
10. **Threat Intelligence (H-ISAC)**
    Actionable insights into current cyber threats, gathered from sources like the

Health Information Sharing and Analysis Center (H-ISAC), used to proactively adjust security defenses.

11. **Zero Trust Architecture (ZTA)**
A security model that assumes no user or device is trusted by default—even inside the network—and enforces strict identity verification and least-privilege access for every request.

12. **Endpoint Resilience**
The ability of hospital endpoints (e.g., workstations, mobile devices, clinical equipment) to resist cyber threats and recover quickly from compromise or malfunction.

13. **Downtime Protocols**
Predefined procedures that guide clinical and administrative staff in continuing safe patient care during IT outages or system failures, often due to cyberattacks.

14. **Security Governance**
The framework of policies, procedures, roles, and controls that direct how cybersecurity is managed within the hospital, ensuring accountability and strategic alignment.

15. **Multifactor Authentication (MFA)**
A security method requiring two or more forms of verification (e.g., password + fingerprint) to access systems, providing stronger protection for sensitive hospital applications.

16. **Data Protection**
Measures taken to ensure the confidentiality, integrity, and availability of patient and hospital data against unauthorized access, disclosure, or destruction.

17. **SIEM Integration**
The implementation of a Security Information and Event Management (SIEM) system that aggregates and analyzes logs from multiple sources to detect and respond to security events.

18. **Cyber Incident Response**
A set of actions taken when a cybersecurity event occurs, including identification, containment, eradication, recovery, and communication across stakeholders.

19. **Microsegmentation**
The practice of dividing hospital networks into smaller, secure zones to limit lateral movement by attackers and contain the impact of a breach.

20. **Behavioral Analytics (UEBA)**
User and Entity Behavior Analytics is a technique that uses machine learning to identify deviations from normal patterns in user behavior, helping detect insider threats and compromised accounts.

Chapter 2: Establish Governance and Security Policies

1. Draft and Update Hospital-Wide IT Security Policies (HIPAA Privacy/Security Rule Alignment)

Governance begins with clearly written, enforceable, and current policies that guide all aspects of IT security within a healthcare environment. In hospitals, IT policies are the formal mechanisms through which security expectations are communicated and compliance is enforced. A hospital CISO must ensure these policies are not only aligned with technical best practices but also with regulatory obligations such as the HIPAA Privacy and Security Rules.

To begin, it's essential to map out a policy framework that covers administrative safeguards (e.g., workforce security, access control), physical safeguards (e.g., device security, facility access), and technical safeguards (e.g., encryption, audit controls). Each category should be addressed with individual policies that are reviewed and updated at least annually.

Policy development should be a cross-functional effort involving IT security, legal, compliance, HR, and clinical leadership. This ensures that policies are relevant, operationally feasible, and enforceable. For example, a password policy may need to consider not only NIST recommendations but also how it will affect fast-paced clinical environments.

Additionally, each policy should contain:

- **Purpose and scope**
- **Roles and responsibilities**
- **Implementation guidelines**
- **Enforcement and sanctions**
- **References to applicable laws and standards**

Every policy should reference HIPAA clauses it supports, such as §164.312(d) for access control or §164.308(a)(1) for risk management. This mapping makes policies easier to defend during audits and OCR investigations.

Finally, maintain version-controlled documentation and implement a policy management system that ensures hospital staff always access the most current version.

2. Ensure Clear Guidelines for EMR Access, BYOD, and Remote Access

Hospitals are unique in the diversity of roles and devices that interact with sensitive data. From physicians accessing EMRs in emergency rooms to billing clerks working remotely during a pandemic, access policies must clearly define **who can access what, from where, and how**.

Start by establishing role-based access control (RBAC) guidelines for the EMR system. Clinical roles (e.g., nurse, radiologist, anesthesiologist) and administrative roles (e.g., billing, scheduling) should have clearly defined access levels that align with the principle of least privilege.

Bring Your Own Device (BYOD) policies are increasingly important as clinicians and administrative staff use personal smartphones, tablets, or laptops to check schedules, emails, and patient updates. BYOD policies must:

- Specify approved device types and operating systems
- Require enrollment in Mobile Device Management (MDM)
- Enforce encryption, screen locks, and remote wipe capabilities
- Prohibit local storage or printing of PHI from personal devices

For **remote access**, whether from home, satellite clinics, or travel, policies must include:

- Use of VPN with multifactor authentication (MFA)
- Session timeouts and auto-disconnects
- Restrictions on downloading or saving files locally
- Auditing and logging requirements

All access policies should be reinforced by mandatory training and acknowledged annually through user agreements.

---

3. Define Emergency Access Procedures for Patient Care Scenarios

In healthcare, access controls must account for life-and-death scenarios. When emergencies occur, standard authentication protocols may delay care, so hospitals must define "break-glass" procedures that allow authorized overrides—while maintaining accountability and traceability.

An effective emergency access policy includes:

- Conditions under which emergency access is permitted (e.g., unconscious patient in trauma bay)
- Authorized personnel eligible for break-glass access
- Temporary override mechanisms within the EMR

- Real-time logging of override events
- Immediate post-event reviews by the security or compliance team

Break-glass events should be monitored for patterns of misuse. If an individual consistently uses emergency access without documentation or proper cause, it should trigger an investigation.

In addition to technical mechanisms, printed quick-reference guides should be available in all clinical areas to remind staff how to initiate emergency access procedures.

Include provisions for extended disasters or outages—such as ransomware attacks—that require prolonged alternative access to patient data through offline backups or paper records. This policy must align with downtime procedures and business continuity planning.

4. Establish Access and Usage Policies for IoMT and Clinical Devices

The proliferation of **Internet of Medical Things (IoMT)** devices—such as smart infusion pumps, networked ventilators, and wireless monitors—has created new challenges for security governance. These devices often operate with minimal human interaction, rely on legacy protocols, and connect to critical care networks, making them high-value targets for attackers.

A formal policy for IoMT and clinical devices should cover:

- Procurement standards including cybersecurity certifications (e.g., UL 2900, FDA premarket guidance)
- Mandatory risk assessments before deployment
- Network segmentation requirements
- Password and firmware management protocols
- Use of secure communication protocols (e.g., TLS 1.2+)
- Logging and monitoring integration with SIEM

Policies must also address maintenance access by biomedical engineers and vendors. Privileged access should be limited, monitored, and time-bound.

Furthermore, disposal policies must ensure that PHI or sensitive configurations are wiped from decommissioned medical devices using NIST 800-88 guidelines or equivalent.

Enforcement of these policies requires collaboration between the CISO, Biomedical Engineering, Facilities, and Clinical Informatics departments.

5. Assign Departmental Compliance Liaisons Across Hospital Units

Central cybersecurity policies can fail without localized enforcement and cultural integration. To bridge this gap, hospitals should implement a **decentralized compliance liaison model**, in which each major department—such as Radiology, ICU, Emergency, and Administration—designates a security liaison.

These liaisons serve as:

- The first point of contact for departmental cybersecurity issues
- Conduits for disseminating policy updates and training reminders
- Collaborators in risk assessments and incident reporting
- Advocates for department-specific cybersecurity needs

The CISO should develop a formal charter for this program and provide training tailored to each liaison's role. Regular meetings or workshops help these liaisons stay informed about policy changes, industry trends, and real-world case studies.

Empowering department-level leaders to enforce and adapt cybersecurity policies creates a **culture of shared responsibility** and vastly improves compliance with minimal resistance.

---

6. Include Clinical and Non-Clinical Stakeholders in Policy Review

Cybersecurity policy creation in hospitals cannot occur in isolation from the broader institutional community. Policies that are drafted without input from the people most affected by them—such as nurses, physicians, medical technicians, administrative assistants, and even maintenance staff—are often met with resistance, confusion, or non-compliance. To be effective, a hospital's cybersecurity governance model must embrace **inclusive policy development and review**, actively engaging both clinical and non-clinical stakeholders.

First, the CISO should identify all relevant stakeholder groups. This includes:

- Clinical roles: physicians, nurses, medical assistants, radiology technicians
- Operational staff: health information management (HIM), admissions, billing
- IT and technical staff: system admins, EMR specialists, network engineers
- Support services: facilities, environmental services, food & nutrition
- Legal and compliance teams
- Human Resources and Training/Education staff

Engagement begins by forming a **Cybersecurity Policy Review Committee** with representation from each major group. This committee should meet regularly—quarterly or biannually—to review proposed policy drafts, assess the impact on workflows, and ensure that terminology and expectations are clearly understood.

For example, a new policy requiring multifactor authentication (MFA) on all systems must be reviewed by clinical leaders to ensure it doesn't disrupt care delivery in high-pressure environments like surgery or trauma. Similarly, administrative leaders may provide critical feedback about the feasibility of access controls on billing software used by rotating contractors.

Some key principles for stakeholder engagement in policy review include:

- **Transparency**: Clearly explain why a policy is needed, what risks it mitigates, and what standards it supports (e.g., HIPAA, NIST, HITECH).
- **Clarity**: Use non-technical language where possible, especially when addressing non-IT audiences.
- **Respect for workflow**: Validate that security requirements do not impose undue burdens or create unsafe clinical workarounds.
- **Feedback loops**: Allow departments to test proposed changes in pilot programs before full implementation.

In addition to formal committees, use tools such as anonymous surveys, roundtable discussions, and department-specific briefings to collect input and build consensus. Feedback gathered through these channels can reveal unintended consequences, such as excessive logout timeouts in charting rooms or difficulties accessing secure messaging platforms on mobile devices.

Once policies are finalized, stakeholders should continue to be part of the **education and communication plan**. Clinical and operational leaders are often more effective at reinforcing policy adherence within their teams than IT or compliance staff. By giving them ownership in the policy development process, you empower them to become cybersecurity advocates.

Finally, all policy revisions should be documented with tracked changes and version control. Include an appendix listing stakeholders involved in the policy's review and development, demonstrating to regulators, auditors, and internal leadership that the policy reflects both **compliance requirements** and **operational realities**.

Inclusion of all stakeholders isn't just good practice—it is essential for real-world adoption and risk reduction. When the people affected by policies help shape them, they are more likely to support, enforce, and advocate for secure behaviors across the hospital.

Chapter 2 Keywords and Definitions

1. **Cybersecurity Governance**
   The structured framework of policies, procedures, and controls that guide the

management of security within a hospital environment. It ensures that risk is managed effectively and aligns security practices with organizational goals and compliance standards.

2. **HIPAA Privacy/Security Rule**
Federal regulations under the Health Insurance Portability and Accountability Act that mandate safeguards to protect the confidentiality, integrity, and availability of protected health information (PHI).

3. **Policy Management System**
A centralized tool or platform used to draft, publish, track, and review cybersecurity policies across the organization. It ensures version control and that staff always access the latest approved documents.

4. **Role-Based Access Control (RBAC)**
A method of restricting system access based on a user's role within the organization. In hospitals, this ensures that clinical and administrative staff access only the systems and data necessary for their duties.

5. **Bring Your Own Device (BYOD)**
A policy that governs how personal devices (smartphones, tablets, laptops) can be securely used by employees to access hospital systems, typically with requirements for MDM, encryption, and usage restrictions.

6. **Mobile Device Management (MDM)**
Technology that allows the CISO to enforce security controls on mobile devices, such as remote wipe, encryption, and app restrictions, to protect PHI and secure hospital networks.

7. **Remote Access Policy**
Rules and requirements for accessing hospital systems from outside the hospital network, often including the use of VPNs, MFA, session timeouts, and monitoring for anomalous behavior.

8. **Emergency Access Procedures (Break-Glass Access)**
Special access privileges granted to authorized personnel during clinical emergencies. These procedures allow for overriding standard access controls to ensure patient safety, with full audit logging.

9. **Internet of Medical Things (IoMT)**
A network of interconnected medical devices that collect and transmit health data. Examples include smart monitors, infusion pumps, and ventilators. These devices require specialized policies for access, updates, and risk management.

10. **Microsegmentation**
A network security practice that divides the hospital's network into isolated segments, limiting movement between them. It's essential for containing threats targeting medical devices or specific departments.

11. **Biomedical Engineering**
A hospital department responsible for maintaining medical equipment. This team plays a critical role in the cybersecurity of IoMT devices, including patching, configuration, and decommissioning.

12. **Compliance Liaison Program**
A decentralized model where each hospital department designates a point-of-

contact responsible for promoting cybersecurity awareness, enforcing policy, and coordinating with the CISO.

13. **Policy Review Committee**
A multidisciplinary group of stakeholders that evaluates new and existing policies to ensure clarity, clinical alignment, and operational feasibility. Includes representatives from clinical, technical, legal, and administrative roles.

14. **Downtime Protocols**
Structured procedures that guide hospital staff on how to continue operations during IT system outages, including alternative access to patient data and communication systems.

15. **Version Control (Policy)**
A documented system that tracks revisions, edits, approvals, and the publishing dates of each cybersecurity policy, ensuring transparency and accountability.

16. **Least Privilege Principle**
A security concept stating that users should only have access to the information and resources necessary for their job functions, minimizing potential exposure and abuse.

17. **Multidisciplinary Collaboration**
The process of including various departments—clinical, IT, compliance, legal, and administration—in developing cybersecurity policies to ensure buy-in and practical implementation.

18. **Access Control Policy**
A documented set of rules governing who can access what data, under which conditions, and through what means, ensuring secure handling of PHI across systems and departments.

19. **Audit Logging**
The process of recording and analyzing user actions within hospital systems, particularly around access to PHI. It is vital for detecting misuse and supporting forensic investigations.

20. **Operational Feasibility**
The practicality of implementing a cybersecurity control or policy without disrupting clinical workflows or reducing the quality of patient care.

Chapter 3: Oversee Risk Management and Assessment Programs

1. Perform Risk Assessments for Departments with High PHI Volume (ER, Cardiology, Oncology)

Hospitals operate as complex ecosystems, but certain departments—such as the Emergency Room (ER), Cardiology, and Oncology—handle disproportionate volumes of protected health information (PHI) and often under time-sensitive conditions. These high-PHI departments are prime targets for cybercriminals due to the sensitivity, volume, and urgency associated with the data they process.

A hospital CISO must begin the risk assessment process by identifying these PHI-intensive areas and mapping their data flows, including how patient information is collected, accessed, stored, and shared. Each of these departments typically relies on integrated medical devices, cloud-based diagnostic platforms, and third-party vendors—all of which increase the attack surface.

In the ER, for example, risk assessments should focus on system availability. Delays or outages in EHR access, triage software, or imaging systems can directly compromise patient outcomes. For Cardiology, where remote telemetry devices and digital ECGs are common, risk assessments must include real-time device communications, vendor software updates, and data integrity. In Oncology, the focus shifts to privacy—especially around treatment plans, genetic testing data, and experimental therapy records that are highly confidential and often shared across research institutions.

Effective assessments in these departments involve:

- Asset inventories and system dependency mapping
- Identification of potential threat vectors (e.g., ransomware, phishing, insider threat)
- Likelihood and impact analysis for each risk
- Consultations with clinical department heads to understand workflows

Results should be documented and translated into actionable mitigation plans, with prioritization based on potential harm to patient care, regulatory exposure, and reputational risk.

2. Identify Risks Tied to Patient Care Interruptions (e.g., Ransomware)

Few threats are more dangerous to a hospital than those that disrupt the delivery of patient care. Unlike other industries, where downtime results in lost revenue, in healthcare it can result in **loss of life**. Cyberattacks like ransomware—which lock users out of systems until a ransom is paid—can completely paralyze clinical workflows, forcing hospitals to divert patients, reschedule surgeries, or revert to paper-based documentation.

A CISO must evaluate all risks that have the potential to cause **care interruptions**, including but not limited to:

- Ransomware and malware infections
- Distributed Denial of Service (DDoS) attacks
- System configuration errors or failed updates
- Unpatched vulnerabilities in core hospital infrastructure

The assessment must begin with an understanding of **care-critical systems**—EHRs, medication administration tools, radiology/PACS, operating room schedulers, and laboratory systems. From there, the analysis must determine:

- How long these systems can be down before care is compromised (Recovery Time Objectives)
- What manual fallback procedures exist, and how reliable they are
- Whether sufficient offline backups and paper protocols are in place

An effective mitigation strategy includes regular backup tests, incident response drills, endpoint hardening, and 24/7 monitoring of abnormal system behavior. Special attention must also be given to the **communication systems**—including phones, pagers, secure messaging, and email—that clinicians use to coordinate care.

Ultimately, any cyber event that can delay diagnoses, treatments, or procedures must be addressed as a top-tier risk.

---

3. Evaluate Cyber Risks Related to Medical Device Interoperability

Medical device interoperability—the ability for devices to exchange and interpret shared data—is a growing necessity in modern hospitals. However, it also introduces new risks as these devices increasingly rely on wireless communication, cloud integration, and vendor-managed interfaces.

From smart infusion pumps to wireless EKGs and portable X-ray machines, these devices are part of the **Internet of Medical Things (IoMT)**. They often run on outdated operating systems, lack encryption, and are rarely patched, making them an attractive target for attackers.

A CISO must assess:

- Whether connected devices are segregated on their own network segments

- The protocols used for device communication (e.g., HL7, DICOM, Bluetooth, Wi-Fi)
- The security controls implemented by vendors (authentication, logging, firmware integrity)
- The potential impact of device failure on patient care

Risk assessments should also review interoperability platforms such as integration engines (e.g., Cloverleaf, Rhapsody), which aggregate and transmit clinical data between systems. A compromise in these platforms can result in widespread data corruption or leakage.

Part of the assessment process should include penetration testing of vendor APIs, evaluations of patch management policies, and strict procurement checklists to ensure new devices meet cybersecurity standards before deployment.

4. Maintain a Risk Register Specific to PHI, Hospital Operations, and Regulatory Exposure

A risk register is a centralized, living document that tracks known cybersecurity risks across the organization. For hospitals, it must capture a broad spectrum of threats: from PHI breaches and insider misuse to system outages and third-party failures.

An effective risk register includes:

- A clear description of each risk
- Source of the risk (department, system, process)
- Likelihood and impact scoring
- Assigned owner(s)
- Current mitigation controls
- Residual risk after controls
- Planned remediation actions and deadlines
- Status updates and revision history

PHI risks should be flagged and monitored closely, especially those involving EHR access, medical imaging systems, and data sent to external providers. Operational risks—such as single points of failure in critical systems—must be equally prioritized. Regulatory risks, including noncompliance with HIPAA, HITECH, or the Joint Commission's cybersecurity elements, must be documented with references to legal consequences and financial penalties.

This register should be reviewed monthly by IT and compliance, and quarterly by executive leadership. It also serves as key evidence during audits or OCR investigations.

5. Involve Compliance Officers and Legal in Risk Mitigation Planning

Risk management in healthcare is not just a technical exercise—it's also a legal and regulatory function. Noncompliance with data protection laws like HIPAA or GDPR can result in significant fines, lawsuits, and public backlash. Therefore, the risk mitigation planning process must involve **compliance and legal teams from the outset**.

Compliance officers provide critical guidance on how identified risks translate into regulatory violations and can help prioritize remediation based on legal exposure. Legal counsel ensures that policies, contracts, and incident response actions are defensible and aligned with both federal and state laws.

Risk mitigation discussions should be formalized through joint working groups or steering committees where cybersecurity, compliance, and legal regularly meet to:

- Review the risk register
- Assign accountability for mitigation plans
- Interpret legal obligations tied to specific vulnerabilities
- Evaluate breach notification procedures and timelines
- Determine acceptable risk thresholds based on business context

This collaboration ensures a balanced risk treatment plan—one that considers technical feasibility, operational impact, and legal defensibility.

6. Conduct HIPAA Security Rule Risk Assessments Annually

HIPAA requires all covered entities and business associates to conduct regular risk assessments under the **HIPAA Security Rule (§164.308(a)(1))**. This is not optional—it is a regulatory obligation and a cornerstone of hospital cybersecurity governance.

The assessment must cover:

- All systems that create, receive, store, or transmit PHI
- Administrative, physical, and technical safeguards
- Likely threats to PHI confidentiality, integrity, and availability
- Existing controls and their effectiveness
- Potential impact of breaches

This process should be documented thoroughly, using structured frameworks such as the **NIST Risk Management Framework (RMF)** or **HHS Security Risk Assessment Tool**. The output should include:

- A documented assessment report
- A remediation roadmap
- Timeframes for implementation
- Metrics for monitoring progress

Annual risk assessments should be supplemented by ad hoc reviews when major changes occur—such as EHR migrations, vendor transitions, or security incidents. Noncompliance with this requirement is one of the most common findings in OCR investigations and should be treated as a strategic priority.

7. Use Structured Risk Frameworks (e.g., NIST, HITRUST, FAIR)

To standardize risk assessment and management, hospitals must adopt structured frameworks that align with regulatory mandates and industry best practices. The use of consistent methodologies enables repeatability, improves risk communication, and provides defensibility during audits or breach investigations.

The **NIST Cybersecurity Framework (CSF)** is one of the most widely adopted models in healthcare. It organizes cybersecurity activities into five core functions—**Identify, Protect, Detect, Respond, and Recover**—and includes subcategories tied to specific controls. The NIST CSF is flexible, scalable, and often mapped directly to HIPAA safeguards.

The **HITRUST CSF** is another popular choice, especially for hospitals seeking third-party certification. It incorporates requirements from HIPAA, NIST, ISO 27001, COBIT, and PCI-DSS into a single integrated framework. HITRUST's control maturity levels provide clear roadmaps for incremental improvement.

For hospitals focusing on quantifying risk in economic terms, the **FAIR (Factor Analysis of Information Risk)** model is ideal. FAIR enables CISOs and executives to understand and compare risks based on financial exposure and probable loss, which is especially useful for insurance or budget justification.

When selecting a framework, consider:

- Organizational maturity and resources
- Regulatory alignment (HIPAA, HITECH)
- Level of executive buy-in required
- Need for external audit or certification

Once a framework is chosen, integrate it into all risk assessment activities. Train staff on its application, embed it into policies and governance documents, and map your risk register and mitigation plans to its domains.

---

8. Prioritize Risks Based on Clinical Impact and Business Continuity

Not all cybersecurity risks are created equal. In a hospital, the **clinical impact** of a system outage or data breach can be far more severe than the technical severity score might suggest. For this reason, risk prioritization must go beyond CVSS ratings or IT-focused metrics.

The prioritization process should begin by identifying systems critical to **clinical care delivery**, such as:

- EHR platforms
- Laboratory information systems
- Pharmacy and medication dispensing systems
- Operating room schedulers
- Telemetry and remote monitoring platforms

Once critical systems are identified, assess risks based on how they could disrupt patient safety, treatment timelines, or compliance with care standards. Risks should be tiered according to:

- Potential for harm or mortality
- Impact on hospital operations (e.g., ER diversion, surgical delays)
- Regulatory violations and legal exposure
- Recovery complexity and time

Collaboration with clinical leadership is essential. For example, a vulnerability in a wireless cardiac monitor may not rank high in a traditional IT scan, but if exploited, it could delay life-saving interventions.

Business continuity is the second lens through which risks must be prioritized. Consider:

- System interdependencies (e.g., how PACS affects radiology and oncology)
- Vendor reliance and failover options
- Staffing and training for manual fallback processes

Prioritized risks must feed into executive-level reporting and budget allocation to ensure timely mitigation.

---

9. Monitor Risk Remediation Progress and Report to Executives

Risk identification is only the first step; successful programs depend on disciplined **risk remediation tracking** and transparent communication with executive leadership.

For each risk logged in the register, assign:

- A remediation owner (e.g., IT Security, Clinical Informatics, Vendor)
- A target resolution date
- Required resources (budget, tools, personnel)

- Dependencies or blockers

Track remediation actions through a centralized dashboard or GRC platform, using traffic-light indicators (Red, Yellow, Green) to show progress status. Include both technical fixes (e.g., patch deployment, network segmentation) and procedural changes (e.g., policy updates, staff training).

Schedule monthly risk review meetings with remediation owners to:

- Validate closure of completed items
- Reassess open items in light of new intelligence
- Escalate stalled actions to leadership

At the executive level, risk summaries should:

- Highlight top 5–10 open risks by criticality
- Show trend lines for residual risk reduction
- Provide business context, such as patient safety implications or financial exposure
- Request strategic decisions for unresolved or accepted risks

Executive buy-in is vital for high-risk issues requiring significant investment or workflow redesign. Use board reports to advocate for staffing, tool acquisition, or architecture redesign.

---

10. Integrate Risk Management into Project and Change Management Processes

Hospitals frequently launch new initiatives—EHR upgrades, telehealth expansion, new imaging platforms, cloud migrations—that can introduce new cyber risks. To avoid surprises, the CISO must integrate risk management into all major **IT project lifecycles and change control processes**.

This starts by embedding cybersecurity into the **Project Management Office (PMO)** workflow. Every major initiative should trigger a **cybersecurity impact assessment**, identifying:

- New data flows or integrations
- Third-party vendors involved
- User access changes
- Potential disruption to existing security controls

Assign security analysts to project teams as dedicated advisors. Their role is to guide secure design decisions, enforce baseline requirements, and conduct risk assessments during development, not after deployment.

Establish a formal **Change Advisory Board (CAB)** that includes cybersecurity review for all proposed changes to:

- System configurations
- Network topology
- Clinical applications
- Data storage and transmission

All changes should be documented with risk ratings, rollback plans, and testing requirements. Urgent changes (e.g., patching an exploited zero-day) should follow a fast-track process but still include risk validation.

This integration ensures cybersecurity is a proactive component of innovation rather than a reactive barrier.

11. Collaborate with IT, Clinical, and Administrative Teams on Risk Ownership

One of the most overlooked yet critical components of effective hospital risk management is the clear assignment of **risk ownership** across all relevant teams. Risk mitigation is not solely the responsibility of the CISO or IT security team—it requires shared accountability across clinical, administrative, and technical stakeholders.

Start by **categorizing risks** based on where they originate and which operational areas they affect:

- IT-driven risks (e.g., unpatched systems, weak authentication)
- Clinical workflow risks (e.g., shared login credentials at nursing stations)
- Administrative risks (e.g., improper handling of PHI in billing offices)
- Vendor-related risks (e.g., third-party EHR plugins or diagnostic tools)

Assign each risk to a **business owner** who understands the impact of the risk and can implement or support mitigation. For example:

- The Director of Radiology should own risks related to PACS access and device security.
- The CNO (Chief Nursing Officer) should co-own risks tied to nursing workflows involving mobile access to the EHR.
- The CIO or IT Director may be responsible for network segmentation or legacy system remediation.

Foster collaboration through cross-functional **risk committees** where issues are tracked, mitigation plans are presented, and timelines are reviewed. These sessions help break down silos and reinforce that cybersecurity is a **shared organizational duty**, not just an IT function.

To support this culture, develop educational resources that explain risk in operational terms, not just technical language. Reinforce how poor risk posture can lead to care delays, legal liability, and reputational damage.

12. Assess Third-Party Risks Including Business Associates and Vendors

Hospitals depend heavily on third-party vendors and **Business Associates (BAs)** for services like billing, transcription, imaging, data storage, and telehealth. These partners often have direct or indirect access to PHI, making third-party risk assessment a cornerstone of cybersecurity strategy.

Start with a **vendor inventory**, identifying all external parties that process or store hospital data. Classify vendors by risk tier (high, medium, low) based on:

- The volume and sensitivity of data accessed
- Whether access is remote or on-site
- Whether the vendor uses subcontractors
- Regulatory and contractual obligations (e.g., BAA signed)

High-risk vendors should undergo **comprehensive security assessments**, including:

- Completion of security questionnaires (based on NIST or HITRUST)
- Review of SOC 2 or ISO 27001 certifications
- Onsite or virtual audits (especially for cloud or critical system vendors)
- Evidence of vulnerability management, incident response, and encryption

In contracts, ensure the inclusion of:

- Data breach notification timelines
- Incident response cooperation clauses
- Right-to-audit provisions
- Termination and data disposal language

Vendor performance should be monitored **continuously**, not just at onboarding. Monitor for:

- Reported data breaches involving the vendor
- Security posture scores (via tools like BitSight or SecurityScorecard)
- Changes in services or infrastructure

Finally, ensure that third-party risk is integrated into the **risk register**, with controls and owners assigned for each vendor relationship. Hospitals are increasingly held accountable for third-party failures, making this a critical focus area.

13. Conduct Periodic Risk Reassessments and Scenario Testing

Risk is not static. New threats, system changes, regulatory updates, and staffing shifts can all affect the hospital's risk profile. Regular **reassessment and scenario-based testing** ensure that the organization adapts to emerging risks and validates the effectiveness of its controls.

Define a **risk reassessment schedule** based on:

- Risk tier (e.g., quarterly for high-risk, annually for low-risk)
- Trigger events (e.g., after a breach, vendor switch, major system upgrade)
- Regulatory mandates (e.g., annual HIPAA Security Rule assessment)

Complement reassessments with **scenario testing**—simulations designed to expose weaknesses in people, processes, and technology. Common test scenarios include:

- Ransomware attack disrupting EHR access
- Insider stealing patient records for fraud
- Supply chain compromise introducing malicious code into PACS
- Email phishing targeting the C-Suite

Each scenario should involve relevant departments (e.g., IT, clinical leadership, legal, PR) and include:

- Realistic threat simulations
- Role-based response expectations
- Incident reporting and communication drills
- Post-exercise reviews and lessons learned

Document the findings and integrate them into your risk register and incident response plans. These exercises improve organizational readiness and expose risks that might not appear in a traditional scan or interview-based assessment.

14. Prepare Risk Reports for the Board and Regulators

Hospital boards and regulatory bodies increasingly expect regular, transparent **risk reporting** from CISOs. These reports should go beyond technical jargon and clearly communicate the **business, operational, and patient safety implications** of cyber risks.

Prepare board-level reports quarterly or biannually, including:

- Top risks and risk categories (e.g., PHI exposure, system availability, vendor risk)

- Residual risk status (after current controls)
- Trends in risk posture over time
- Key incidents or near-misses
- High-priority mitigation plans and barriers to resolution
- Required executive decisions or support

Use visuals like:

- Risk heat maps
- Risk trajectory graphs
- Comparative risk exposure against peer institutions
- Risk-to-strategy alignment (e.g., how cyber investments protect clinical outcomes)

Reports to regulators (e.g., HHS OCR, state health departments) must adhere to **HIPAA documentation standards**, with detailed:

- Risk analysis findings
- Action plans
- Implementation status
- Policy documentation
- Evidence of staff training and enforcement

Proactive communication with regulators following an incident (e.g., ransomware breach) often mitigates enforcement severity. Demonstrating that a formal, risk-based security program was in place is your best defense during audits and investigations.

Chapter 3 Keywords and Definitions

1. **Risk Assessment**
   A systematic process of identifying and evaluating potential threats to hospital systems, data, and patient safety, along with the likelihood and impact of those threats.
2. **Protected Health Information (PHI)**
   Any individually identifiable health information, such as medical records, billing data, or treatment histories, that is protected under HIPAA.
3. **Care Interruption Risk**
   Cyber threats that disrupt clinical operations, such as ransomware attacks that render systems like EHRs inaccessible, potentially impacting patient safety and outcomes.
4. **Medical Device Interoperability**
   The ability of medical devices to communicate and operate with other hospital systems. It introduces risks when those devices lack strong cybersecurity controls.

5. **Risk Register**
   A centralized document or platform that tracks known cyber risks, including their severity, ownership, mitigation strategies, and current status.
6. **HIPAA Security Rule**
   A federal regulation requiring covered entities to conduct regular risk assessments and implement safeguards to protect the confidentiality, integrity, and availability of ePHI.
7. **NIST Cybersecurity Framework (CSF)**
   A voluntary framework consisting of standards and best practices to manage cybersecurity risk. Widely adopted in healthcare to structure risk management programs.
8. **HITRUST CSF**
   A certifiable security and privacy framework that incorporates healthcare-specific regulations like HIPAA and maps to multiple industry standards (NIST, ISO, etc.).
9. **FAIR Model (Factor Analysis of Information Risk)**
   A quantitative risk analysis model used to measure and compare cybersecurity risks in financial terms, aiding executive decision-making.
10. **Risk Prioritization**
    The process of ranking risks based on their potential impact to clinical outcomes, hospital operations, regulatory compliance, and patient safety.
11. **Business Continuity Planning (BCP)**
    Strategies to ensure hospital operations can continue during and after a disruption, including system outages caused by cyberattacks.
12. **Remediation Tracking**
    Monitoring the progress of corrective actions assigned to mitigate risks. This includes assigning owners, setting deadlines, and reporting status to leadership.
13. **Change Advisory Board (CAB)**
    A governance body that reviews proposed changes to hospital systems and ensures cybersecurity risks are evaluated before implementation.
14. **Cybersecurity Impact Assessment**
    A formal analysis of how a new project, technology, or vendor might introduce risks to the hospital's security posture and PHI protection.
15. **Risk Ownership**
    The assignment of responsibility for addressing specific risks to individuals or departments that can influence or resolve them.
16. **Third-Party Risk Management**
    The process of assessing and monitoring the security practices of vendors and business associates who have access to hospital systems or data.
17. **Business Associate Agreement (BAA)**
    A legally required contract between a covered entity and a third party that outlines the responsibilities for safeguarding PHI under HIPAA.
18. **Scenario-Based Testing**
    Simulated exercises that evaluate how well the hospital can respond to specific cybersecurity threats, such as ransomware or insider misuse.

19. **Board Reporting**

The process of presenting cybersecurity risk information to hospital executives and board members in clear, strategic, and business-relevant terms.

20. **Regulatory Risk Reporting**

Documented reports and evidence submitted to government agencies (e.g., HHS OCR) to demonstrate compliance with security standards and incident response protocols.

Chapter 4: Lead Incident Response Planning and Execution

1. Maintain a Healthcare-Specific IR Playbook for PHI Breaches

A well-documented and regularly updated **Incident Response (IR) playbook** is one of the most essential tools in the hospital CISO's arsenal. Unlike generalized IR plans, a healthcare-specific playbook must prioritize **Protected Health Information (PHI)** and account for the operational complexity of clinical environments.

This playbook should address all phases of the **NIST Incident Response Lifecycle**: preparation, detection and analysis, containment, eradication and recovery, and post-incident activities. Each phase should be customized with healthcare-relevant scenarios—such as unauthorized EMR access, ransomware infections, or email phishing that leads to credential theft.

Key components of a healthcare IR playbook include:

- A PHI-specific breach response checklist
- Definitions and classification of incident severity levels
- Designated incident response team members (IR Team/CIRT)
- Roles for IT, compliance, legal, communications, and clinical leadership
- Step-by-step escalation matrix for internal and regulatory reporting
- Secure communication protocols during an active incident

Regular review and revision are vital. The playbook should be updated:

- Annually, at minimum
- After significant incidents or system upgrades
- Following regulatory updates (e.g., changes in HIPAA breach notification rules)

Finally, the playbook should be available both digitally and in hard copy across key hospital departments, ensuring rapid access even during major system outages.

2. Define 'Code Cyber' Response Levels and Escalation Procedures

In the clinical world, standardized codes (e.g., Code Blue, Code Red) enable immediate, coordinated responses to emergencies. The same concept can be applied to cybersecurity. Implementing a **"Code Cyber" system** empowers staff across departments to recognize and respond appropriately to cyber threats with clear levels of urgency.

The CISO should lead the creation of a tiered alert system, such as:

- **Code Cyber - Green**: Low-risk events (e.g., isolated phishing email)
- **Code Cyber - Yellow**: Moderate events with limited operational impact (e.g., malware on a nurse station workstation)
- **Code Cyber - Red**: High-severity incidents (e.g., ransomware, EHR compromise, insider exfiltration)

Each level must include defined **response protocols**, including:

- Notification trees (e.g., SOC, IT, clinical managers, CISO, CEO)
- Activation of the IR Team
- Communication protocols, including alternatives if email or VoIP is affected
- Isolation procedures (e.g., network segmentation or endpoint quarantine)

Escalation thresholds should be well-defined to avoid delay. For example, multiple failed login attempts across multiple domains within 5 minutes might escalate from Code Yellow to Red.

To operationalize the program:

- Train department heads and shift leads on their responsibilities per alert level
- Conduct awareness campaigns to introduce the "Code Cyber" system to all staff
- Integrate the code system into hospital paging, alerting apps, or mass notification systems

A "Code Cyber" system simplifies incident recognition and triggers faster, more coordinated responses across clinical and administrative environments.

---

3. Coordinate with Clinical Leads for Downtime Protocols During Cyber Events

When cyber incidents impact system availability—especially core platforms like EHRs, PACS, or scheduling systems—the risk to patient care increases dramatically. The CISO must work closely with **clinical leadership** to ensure that downtime protocols are not only documented but regularly practiced and kept up to date.

Downtime protocols should be co-developed with:

- Chief Nursing Officer (CNO)
- Chief Medical Information Officer (CMIO)
- Department managers (e.g., ICU, ED, Radiology, Surgery)

Each department should have:

- Clear procedures for switching to paper documentation
- Backup systems or offline databases for critical patient data
- Protocols for ordering tests, medications, or procedures manually
- Policies for reconciling paper and digital records post-outage
- Identification of critical workflows that require prioritized recovery

Additionally, consider establishing "downtime kits" in high-volume units, including:

- Pre-printed forms for orders, vitals, medication administration
- Quick guides for clinicians on manual processes
- Contact lists for escalation and IT assistance

Testing of downtime protocols should be incorporated into hospital-wide disaster recovery drills. Just as hospitals test fire response or mass casualty readiness, they must simulate EHR outages to verify staff readiness.

4. Ensure Rapid EHR Access Recovery Procedures Are Tested Quarterly

Given that the **Electronic Health Record (EHR)** is the nerve center of modern clinical operations, restoring its availability after a cyber incident is paramount. Hospitals must treat EHR recovery not only as a technical process but as a clinical imperative.

Quarterly **EHR recovery drills** are essential for:

- Validating the recovery time objective (RTO) and recovery point objective (RPO)
- Confirming the integrity of backups
- Practicing system failover and failback procedures
- Ensuring that system dependencies (e.g., lab results, pharmacy orders) reconnect properly

These tests should simulate:

- Full system failure with manual restart
- Restoration from immutable or offline backups
- Integration reboots for third-party modules (e.g., imaging systems, alerts)

IT teams should conduct these tests in collaboration with clinical users to ensure restored systems function as expected from the end-user perspective. This is especially important for:

- Order entry systems
- Patient chart views
- Medication administration records

Include post-test reports identifying:

- Downtime duration
- Errors encountered
- Time to full recovery
- Recommendations for improvement

Documenting these results supports both **regulatory compliance** and internal audit readiness.

---

5. Conduct Simulated Phishing-Based Breach Drills with Staff

Email phishing remains one of the most common—and successful—entry points for healthcare cyberattacks. The CISO must implement an ongoing program of **simulated phishing exercises**, specifically designed to raise awareness, test user behavior, and evaluate incident response.

Key components of a phishing simulation program include:

- Regular campaigns using varied phishing techniques (credential harvesters, fake invoice lures, spoofed internal senders)
- Targeted simulations for high-risk roles (finance, IT, C-suite, physicians)
- Tracking metrics like open rate, click rate, and credential submission rate
- Follow-up training for users who fail simulations

However, simulations should go beyond user testing—they must also evaluate **technical and procedural response**:

- How quickly does the SOC detect the simulated breach?
- Do users report phishing attempts to the security team?
- Are email filters and DLP tools catching malicious payloads?
- Is the IR playbook activated when a "breach" is simulated?

After-action reviews should be conducted with stakeholders, highlighting:

- Strengths and weaknesses
- Opportunities to improve training
- Updates needed for playbooks or detection tools

These drills normalize cybersecurity vigilance and make the hospital environment more resilient to real phishing attacks.

---

6. Involve Patient Privacy and Legal Teams in Breach Notification Workflows

HIPAA mandates strict timelines and protocols for notifying affected individuals, regulators, and sometimes the media in the event of a PHI breach. These rules must be embedded into the hospital's **incident response workflows**, with clear roles for the **Patient Privacy Officer** and **Legal Counsel**.

Responsibilities include:

- Determining whether an incident meets the threshold for breach notification
- Initiating risk of harm assessments (e.g., what type of PHI was exposed, to whom, and for how long)
- Drafting regulatory and patient-facing notification letters
- Ensuring that OCR and state-level notifications are submitted within required timeframes (typically within 60 days)
- Coordinating with PR teams for public statements, when needed

Legal teams must also:

- Ensure breach response aligns with applicable state privacy laws
- Preserve forensic evidence and documentation in case of litigation
- Review contractual breach obligations with vendors or business associates

Proactive planning avoids delays and ensures that hospitals meet both their **legal obligations** and their **ethical commitment to transparency** with patients.

7. Integrate Cybersecurity into the Hospital's Emergency Management Plan

In modern healthcare environments, **cybersecurity incidents are no longer IT-only emergencies**—they are full-blown operational crises that must be integrated into the hospital's all-hazards Emergency Management Plan (EMP). Whether it's a ransomware attack, a denial-of-service assault, or a data breach disrupting care delivery, the implications span clinical, operational, legal, and reputational domains.

To align cybersecurity with emergency preparedness:

- Incorporate "cybersecurity incident" scenarios into the hospital's **Hazard Vulnerability Analysis (HVA)**
- Coordinate with the **Emergency Management Committee** to define specific response roles and responsibilities
- Align the cybersecurity IR plan with **Incident Command System (ICS)** structures already in place for mass casualty, fire, or utility failure events

ICS roles should include:

- **Incident Commander (often the CIO or CISO)**
- **Operations Section Chief (typically IT or security lead)**
- **Public Information Officer (PIO)**
- **Liaison Officer (legal, clinical leadership, and vendors)**

Cyber-specific responsibilities must be defined and rehearsed, including:

- How cyber events are declared and escalated in ICS format
- How communication is maintained when digital platforms are offline
- How collaboration between IT, nursing, and leadership occurs under pressure

By embedding cybersecurity into emergency preparedness, the hospital becomes better equipped to handle multi-layered crises where clinical and IT systems converge.

---

8. Define Communication Protocols for Internal and External Stakeholders

During a cyber incident, communication is one of the most critical—and fragile—components of response. Hospitals must predefine **secure, redundant, and role-based communication protocols** for both internal and external stakeholders.

Internal communications should address:

- Which platforms are used (e.g., encrypted messaging apps, backup radios, whiteboards in command centers)
- Who initiates notifications and at what thresholds
- Message templates for system status updates, containment actions, and reassurances

External communications include:

- Vendor coordination for systems under third-party management (e.g., EHR hosting or imaging cloud platforms)
- Legal counsel for breach notifications and regulatory engagement
- Media communications coordinated through a designated **PIO (Public Information Officer)**

Hospitals must also define **"off-band" communication channels** in case of full network outages, such as:

- Burner phones for IT and clinical leaders
- Hardcopy phone trees stored in command binders
- Ham radios or satellite phones for rural hospitals

Communication protocols must also account for:

- Patient-facing notifications if appointments, surgeries, or test results are delayed
- Contacting external agencies like the **FBI, HHS OCR, or local law enforcement**
- Updating cyber insurance carriers promptly to initiate claim processes

Clear, calm, and timely communication reduces panic, preserves public trust, and accelerates resolution.

9. Coordinate Digital Forensics and Evidence Preservation

A successful cyber incident response doesn't end when systems are restored. In healthcare, it's vital to preserve forensic evidence to determine root cause, assess scope, support legal actions, and comply with breach notification rules.

The CISO must ensure that digital forensics procedures are built into the IR plan, including:

- Immediate collection of volatile data (e.g., memory dumps, system states)
- Preservation of logs from SIEMs, firewalls, EDR, and authentication systems
- Isolation—not wiping—of compromised endpoints for forensic imaging
- Chain of custody documentation to maintain legal admissibility

Hospitals should establish **partnerships with digital forensics firms** in advance, defining SLAs for onsite response. Internal IT teams must also be trained in first-responder tasks, such as:

- Quarantining affected devices
- Taking screenshots or video captures of suspicious activities
- Extracting logs before log rotation deletes critical evidence

Forensic outcomes support:

- Root cause analysis
- Identification of affected systems and data sets
- Regulatory reporting narratives
- Future risk mitigation

Additionally, ensure that forensic data is stored securely and is inaccessible to unauthorized staff to avoid contamination or accidental deletion.

10. Conduct Post-Incident Reviews and Lessons Learned Exercises

Every cyber incident—whether real or simulated—should be treated as a learning opportunity. The post-incident review (PIR) process is critical for continuous improvement and long-term resilience. CISOs must formalize this process with both technical and clinical stakeholders.

Post-incident activities should occur **within 1–2 weeks** of an event or drill and should include:

- A timeline of the incident from detection to resolution
- Key actions taken and their effectiveness
- Gaps identified in technology, communication, or workflow
- Recovery timeline vs. expectations (RTO/RPO)
- Clinical and patient safety impact assessments
- Review of legal and compliance outcomes

Host a **lessons learned meeting** with representation from:

- IT and cybersecurity
- Nursing and clinical leadership
- Compliance and privacy
- Legal and communications
- Vendor management, if third parties were involved

Outputs from the PIR should be documented in an internal report that feeds into:

- Updates to the incident response playbook
- Training improvements
- System enhancements or architectural changes
- Audit trail for executive and regulatory review

Finally, celebrate successes. Recognizing staff who contributed to swift containment or clever mitigation reinforces positive behavior and strengthens the cybersecurity culture.

Chapter 4 Keywords and Definitions

- **Incident Response (IR) Playbook**
  A detailed, role-based guide outlining procedures to detect, respond to, and recover from cybersecurity incidents. In hospitals, it includes workflows for PHI breaches, EHR outages, and clinical system disruptions.
- **Protected Health Information (PHI)**
  Individually identifiable health data that is protected under HIPAA. Includes patient records, test results, billing data, and more. Must be safeguarded during and after incidents.

- **Code Cyber**
  A hospital-specific escalation system that categorizes the severity of a cybersecurity incident (e.g., Green, Yellow, Red) and triggers predefined response procedures across departments.
- **Downtime Protocols**
  Documented fallback procedures for clinical and administrative operations during system outages. Include manual charting, paper orders, and offline access methods.
- **Electronic Health Record (EHR) Recovery**
  The process of restoring access to the EHR system following an outage or attack. Requires tested backup strategies, failover procedures, and validation by clinical users.
- **Phishing Simulation**
  A training exercise where staff receive simulated malicious emails to test awareness, reporting behavior, and overall readiness to resist real phishing attacks.
- **Security Operations Center (SOC)**
  The team responsible for real-time monitoring and response to cybersecurity threats. In hospitals, the SOC must detect anomalies in clinical systems and infrastructure.
- **Patient Privacy Officer**
  A designated compliance leader responsible for assessing privacy risks and managing breach notification requirements under HIPAA and state laws.
- **Legal and Regulatory Coordination**
  The involvement of internal legal counsel and compliance staff in determining breach classification, notification procedures, and evidence preservation to meet federal and state requirements.
- **Emergency Management Plan (EMP)**
  A comprehensive strategy outlining how the hospital responds to disasters, including cybersecurity events. Incorporates the Incident Command System (ICS) framework.
- **Incident Command System (ICS)**
  A standardized structure for emergency response used in hospitals. It includes defined roles such as Incident Commander and Public Information Officer during a crisis.
- **Communication Protocols**
  Predefined methods and platforms for internal and external messaging during a cybersecurity event, including fallback systems if networks are down.
- **Off-Band Communication**
  Secure, alternative communication channels (e.g., radios, burner phones) used when standard communication systems are compromised or unavailable.
- **Digital Forensics**
  The practice of collecting, analyzing, and preserving digital evidence following a cyber incident. Supports root cause analysis, compliance, and legal proceedings.

- **Chain of Custody**
  A documented process that tracks the handling of digital evidence to ensure its integrity and admissibility in legal investigations.
- **Post-Incident Review (PIR)**
  A formal evaluation of how a cybersecurity incident was handled, including what worked, what failed, and how to improve future response.
- **Lessons Learned Exercise**
  A collaborative debriefing session after an incident or simulation to capture insights, update response plans, and reinforce successful practices.
- **Root Cause Analysis**
  The process of identifying the fundamental reasons an incident occurred, including technical failures, policy gaps, or user behavior.
- **Simulated Breach Drill**
  A practice scenario that mimics a real cyberattack, used to test hospital readiness, validate response playbooks, and train staff under pressure.
- **Breach Notification Requirements**
  Legal obligations under HIPAA and state laws to inform affected individuals and regulators when a breach of PHI occurs.

Chapter 5: Conduct Regular Security Audits and Compliance Reviews

1. Conduct Internal HIPAA Security Audits and Policy Adherence Checks

For hospital CISOs, internal **HIPAA Security Rule** audits are a foundational element of governance and risk management. These audits provide insight into whether administrative, technical, and physical safeguards are in place and functioning effectively to protect **Protected Health Information (PHI)**.

HIPAA Security audits should be conducted annually at minimum, with more frequent reviews for high-risk departments or after significant IT changes. These audits typically include:

- Verification of risk assessment documentation and updates
- Reviews of access control mechanisms (e.g., role-based access, password policies)
- Inspection of encryption policies for PHI in transit and at rest
- Evaluation of contingency plans, including data backup and recovery strategies
- Evidence that workstation security, facility access controls, and device sanitation processes are being followed

To support these efforts, develop a comprehensive **HIPAA audit checklist** that maps internal policies to specific HIPAA requirements (e.g., §164.308, §164.312). Each control should be tested using both documentation review and live validation (e.g., system checks, staff interviews, observation).

In addition to technical controls, CISOs must assess **policy adherence** across clinical and administrative units. For example, is PHI ever left unattended at nursing stations? Are printed patient lists disposed of securely? Are staff routinely locking screens before walking away?

Audit findings should be documented in a structured report that includes:

- Identified gaps or violations
- Risk severity ratings
- Assigned action items
- Remediation timelines
- Evidence of corrective action

These findings must be tracked in a governance dashboard and reported to the compliance office and executive leadership, forming the foundation for ongoing risk mitigation.

2. Audit Clinician Access Logs to Detect Snooping or Abuse

One of the most common—and damaging—forms of internal abuse in hospitals is **inappropriate access to patient records**. This includes "snooping" (e.g., viewing a celebrity or colleague's chart without a clinical reason), accessing one's own medical records, or pulling PHI for malicious purposes such as identity theft.

To prevent and detect this behavior, the CISO must implement and oversee **regular audits of clinician access logs**, especially in high-volume and high-sensitivity areas such as:

- Emergency Department
- Labor and Delivery
- Behavioral Health
- Oncology
- VIP or high-profile patient care units

Logs should be reviewed for red flags such as:

- Users accessing large volumes of records outside their assigned patients
- Access outside of scheduled shifts
- Repeated access to records with no accompanying documentation
- Use of generic or shared logins
- Unauthorized use of "break-the-glass" emergency access

Automated tools like **User and Entity Behavior Analytics (UEBA)** or purpose-built platforms (e.g., FairWarning, Protenus) can help flag anomalies in near real-time and reduce the burden of manual review.

Findings must be:

- Logged and tracked in the compliance risk register
- Investigated with assistance from HR and department leadership
- Followed by coaching, training, or disciplinary action depending on severity

Additionally, education programs should emphasize that all system activity is logged and monitored, reinforcing a **culture of accountability** and discouraging casual or intentional misuse.

3. Review Remote Access by Contractors and Medical Students

In academic and multi-site healthcare systems, **remote access** is a necessary part of operations—but it introduces significant risk, particularly when granted to individuals outside full-time employment such as contractors, vendors, residents, and medical students.

Hospitals must maintain a **centralized inventory** of all remote access users and the systems they can reach, including:

- EHR portals for rotating clinicians
- VPN tunnels for IT vendors and biomedical engineers
- Cloud-based research systems accessed by academic partners
- Secure email and document-sharing platforms

Access reviews should be conducted quarterly and include:

- Verification that each user still requires access
- Documentation of the requestor, authorizer, and reason for access
- Review of session logs for suspicious activity or policy violations
- Comparison of access privileges to the principle of least privilege

Expired accounts must be promptly deactivated. Medical students and rotating residents often complete their clinical time but retain lingering access, presenting serious compliance and privacy risks.

For high-privilege accounts, such as IT contractors or third-party EHR admins, consider:

- Limiting access windows to specific times and durations
- Using **Privileged Access Management (PAM)** tools to issue just-in-time credentials
- Requiring session recordings or command logging

Every remote user must complete security training and sign acceptable use policies that outline monitoring, expectations, and consequences for abuse.

---

4. Validate System Logs for EHR, PACS, and Lab Systems

System logs are a goldmine of forensic, compliance, and security data—if properly collected, retained, and reviewed. The CISO must ensure that logs from critical systems, especially those that manage PHI, are **configured correctly and regularly validated**.

Key systems include:

- **Electronic Health Record (EHR)**: Tracks all user activity—logins, chart access, orders, and edits

- **Picture Archiving and Communication System (PACS)**: Manages access to medical imaging data
- **Laboratory Information System (LIS)**: Handles diagnostic results and test orders

Effective log validation involves:

- Ensuring that audit logs are enabled and configured per best practices
- Verifying time synchronization via NTP across all systems
- Confirming log retention periods meet HIPAA (minimum 6 years for relevant data)
- Checking for log integrity and protection against tampering
- Validating that logs are being forwarded to a **Security Information and Event Management (SIEM)** system for analysis

Sample log reviews should be conducted regularly, focusing on:

- Administrative privilege usage
- Failed login attempts
- Break-glass or override actions
- Bulk data exports or print jobs

Gaps in log collection or integrity must be documented and corrected. System owners should be trained on the importance of logging as both a **compliance requirement and security control**.

---

5. Align with CMS, OCR, and Joint Commission Compliance Frameworks

Hospital cybersecurity governance must align not only with HIPAA but also with other **regulatory and accrediting bodies**, including:

- **Centers for Medicare & Medicaid Services (CMS)**
- **Office for Civil Rights (OCR)**
- **The Joint Commission (TJC)**

Each organization evaluates cybersecurity through a different lens:

- **CMS** may assess electronic data handling as part of Conditions of Participation or Meaningful Use/Promoting Interoperability programs.
- **OCR** oversees HIPAA compliance, focusing on documentation of risk assessments, breach notification, and safeguard enforcement.
- **The Joint Commission** includes cybersecurity preparedness in Environment of Care and Information Management standards, emphasizing patient safety.

To maintain alignment:

- Map internal controls and audit programs to the specific standards of each organization
- Track survey and audit readiness checklists
- Review policy documentation to ensure cross-referenced support of CMS/TJC/OCR expectations
- Include representatives from Quality and Accreditation teams in cybersecurity planning and audits

During accreditation cycles or OCR investigations, your ability to **demonstrate control maturity**—supported by policies, metrics, and audit trails—can significantly influence outcomes.

6. Coordinate with Internal Audit or Third-Party Compliance Consultants

While internal cybersecurity audits form the foundation of continuous compliance, **independent validation** by internal auditors or third-party consultants strengthens the hospital's governance posture and lends credibility to risk management practices. This coordination provides objective oversight, uncovers blind spots, and ensures that cybersecurity controls are functioning as designed.

Internal audit teams often reside within the **finance or compliance department** and typically follow structured, risk-based audit schedules. The CISO should proactively collaborate with this team to:

- Define the cybersecurity audit scope (e.g., access controls, vendor risk, data integrity)
- Provide input on risk assessments and previous audit findings
- Facilitate access to documentation, systems, and staff for audit interviews
- Align findings with enterprise risk management and governance reporting

An effective partnership with internal audit also helps align cybersecurity with **corporate compliance, financial risk**, and **enterprise risk management (ERM)** objectives. Their reports are often reviewed by the hospital board or audit committee, making them essential communication tools for the CISO.

For more specialized or high-risk areas, hospitals often engage **third-party cybersecurity or compliance firms**. These external consultants bring industry expertise, fresh perspectives, and benchmarking capabilities. Common use cases include:

- Pre-OCR HIPAA Security Rule assessments
- HITRUST certification readiness
- Network penetration testing and red team exercises
- Cloud security configuration reviews
- Medical device (IoMT) security audits

When working with third parties, it is essential to:

- Establish clear contractual expectations, including scope, deliverables, and timelines
- Require nondisclosure agreements and data handling controls
- Provide access to only the systems and data needed for the assessment
- Review draft findings collaboratively to ensure accuracy before finalization

Audit outcomes—whether internal or external—must be translated into **corrective action plans (CAPs)** with:

- Clear ownership
- Timelines and milestones
- Integration into the risk register
- Follow-up verification cycles

Lastly, the CISO should present audit summaries and CAP progress to the hospital's **governance committees, privacy boards, and executive leadership**. This ensures alignment on institutional priorities and provides a structured, defensible narrative for compliance oversight bodies.

By embedding regular audits into the cybersecurity lifecycle and partnering across departments and with external experts, the CISO helps build a **culture of accountability, transparency, and continuous improvement**.

Chapter 5 Keywords and Definitions

- **HIPAA Security Rule Audit**
  A formal evaluation of a hospital's compliance with the administrative, technical, and physical safeguards mandated by the HIPAA Security Rule to protect electronic protected health information (ePHI).
- **Policy Adherence Check**
  The process of verifying whether hospital staff and systems are following established cybersecurity and privacy policies, such as password protocols, screen lock usage, and data disposal procedures.
- **Access Log Auditing**
  The review of system logs to track and analyze user activity, helping identify unauthorized or inappropriate access to patient records and sensitive systems.
- **Snooping Detection**
  The process of identifying staff who access patient information without a legitimate clinical or administrative reason—often involving high-profile individuals or coworkers.
- **Remote Access Review**
  A structured evaluation of external access to hospital systems by vendors,

contractors, and students to ensure security measures are enforced and least privilege is maintained.

- **Privileged Access Management (PAM)**
A security strategy and set of tools designed to control and monitor access to systems by users with elevated permissions, such as IT contractors or database administrators.

- **System Log Validation**
The process of confirming that security logs from critical hospital systems (EHR, PACS, LIS) are properly collected, retained, and analyzed for anomalies and incidents.

- **Security Information and Event Management (SIEM)**
A centralized platform that aggregates, analyzes, and alerts on security-related logs and events, enabling real-time threat detection and incident response.

- **Break-the-Glass Access**
A special override access method used in emergencies, allowing clinicians to bypass standard controls for patient care. Logs of such access must be reviewed for abuse.

- **Joint Commission (TJC) Cybersecurity Standards**
Guidelines established by The Joint Commission to ensure hospitals include cybersecurity readiness in their accreditation evaluations, particularly regarding patient safety.

- **Office for Civil Rights (OCR)**
The federal agency responsible for enforcing HIPAA compliance. OCR conducts audits and investigations of breaches involving PHI.

- **CMS Promoting Interoperability**
A Centers for Medicare & Medicaid Services program that incentivizes the secure and meaningful use of EHRs. Hospitals must demonstrate appropriate data handling and access controls.

- **Corrective Action Plan (CAP)**
A documented response to an audit finding or incident, outlining steps to remediate deficiencies, prevent recurrence, and monitor implementation.

- **Compliance Framework Alignment**
The practice of mapping hospital cybersecurity policies and controls to regulatory standards from bodies such as CMS, OCR, and TJC to ensure full-spectrum compliance.

- **Internal Audit Coordination**
Collaboration between the CISO and hospital's internal audit team to ensure cybersecurity risks are evaluated, documented, and integrated into organizational risk management.

- **Third-Party Compliance Consultant**
An external cybersecurity or compliance firm hired to conduct specialized assessments, provide unbiased insight, or prepare for audits and certifications.

- **Least Privilege Principle**
A foundational security concept stating that users should only have access to the data and systems necessary for their job function, reducing the risk of misuse or compromise.

- **Clinical System Audit**
  A security and compliance review of systems integral to patient care, such as EHR, PACS, and LIS, to ensure proper access control, logging, and data integrity.
- **Audit Trail**
  A recorded history of access and activity across systems, used for forensic investigation, regulatory compliance, and policy enforcement.
- **Risk Register Integration**
  The practice of adding audit findings and security issues into the hospital's master risk register to track ownership, remediation progress, and impact.

Chapter 6: Report to Executive Leadership and Hospital Board

1. Provide Dashboards Summarizing PHI Breach Risks and HIPAA Compliance

Executive leaders and board members need **clear, concise, and data-driven summaries** of cyber risk to make informed strategic decisions. For CISOs, this begins with designing and delivering **customized cybersecurity dashboards** that highlight Protected Health Information (PHI) exposure and HIPAA compliance.

These dashboards should prioritize **visual storytelling** over technical jargon. Use data visualizations to communicate risk posture, including:

- Total number of PHI-related incidents by category (e.g., snooping, unauthorized disclosure, ransomware)
- Percentage of systems audited for HIPAA compliance in the last quarter
- Number of open vs. closed corrective actions linked to HIPAA safeguard gaps
- Top 5 HIPAA-related risks from your risk register

Executive dashboards should be updated monthly or quarterly, depending on the audience, and must:

- Include red-yellow-green (RYG) indicators for risk status
- Display metrics on risk trends (e.g., breaches increasing/decreasing)
- Map risks to business units or system owners
- Show the current state of HIPAA Security Rule compliance (e.g., access control, audit logging, data integrity)

Use narrative summaries alongside data to highlight:

- Actions taken since the last report
- Areas of emerging concern (e.g., new phishing campaigns)
- Strategic decisions needed (e.g., funding approval for a DLP system)

Effective dashboards empower the board to engage in **risk-informed decision-making** and demonstrate that cybersecurity oversight is integrated into hospital governance.

2. Translate Cyber Risks into Impacts on Patient Safety and Care Delivery

For non-technical stakeholders, cybersecurity must be presented in a context they understand: **patient safety and operational continuity**. The CISO must regularly translate cyber risks into **clinical impact scenarios** to show how threats can disrupt or degrade care delivery.

Use specific, real-world examples:

- How a ransomware attack on the EHR delayed stroke treatment in the ER
- How a misconfigured PACS system exposed radiology images and created legal risk
- How unauthorized access to a VIP patient's chart created a PR crisis and legal liability

Frame risks around the **care continuum**, such as:

- Diagnosis delays due to lab or imaging outages
- Medication errors from system downtimes
- Missed follow-ups from corrupted patient scheduling systems

Use quantitative data wherever possible:

- Estimated number of patient encounters impacted by downtime
- Lost operating room hours due to system unavailability
- Average response times to clinical incidents tied to cybersecurity events

Collaborate with the **Chief Medical Officer (CMO), Chief Nursing Officer (CNO), and Patient Safety Officer** to validate and frame these scenarios. When possible, create visual "risk journeys" that map the patient's experience during an incident to show operational breakdowns caused by security gaps.

This approach reinforces that cybersecurity is **not just about data**—it's about protecting lives and maintaining trust in the healthcare system.

---

3. Deliver Incident Updates Tied to Hospital Operations (e.g., System Outages)

When cyber incidents occur—whether real breaches or near-misses—executive leaders must be briefed quickly and accurately on the **operational impact, containment progress, and strategic response**.

A well-structured incident update includes:

- Date/time of the incident and detection
- Systems or departments affected
- Current containment status
- Business operations impacted (e.g., surgery delays, ER reroutes)

- Estimated time to full recovery (RTO) and data recovery status (RPO)
- Preliminary root cause and lessons learned
- Regulatory or legal implications
- Communication actions taken (internal/external)

Use an **incident scorecard** format that breaks down:

- Incident severity level (low, moderate, critical)
- Functional domains impacted (clinical, administrative, financial)
- Recovery metrics (MTTD—mean time to detect; MTTR—mean time to recover)

Ensure updates are clear and tailored for **executive consumption**—avoid overloading them with technical details, and focus instead on business continuity and patient impact.

Provide follow-ups during the incident, as well as a **post-incident summary** during governance or board meetings. Tie each incident back to larger trends (e.g., increase in phishing attacks) and link them to strategic risk priorities and mitigation plans.

---

4. Present Ransomware Readiness Metrics and Drills

Ransomware is one of the most critical and visible threats facing hospitals. Boards and leadership need assurance that the organization is **actively preparing for, detecting, and responding to ransomware scenarios.**

Present ransomware readiness using **structured metrics**, such as:

- Number and type of ransomware drills conducted per year
- Results of tabletop exercises with clinical leadership
- Recovery time after mock EHR outages
- Frequency and outcomes of backup restoration tests
- MFA adoption rates for remote access and privileged accounts
- Percentage of staff who failed recent phishing simulations

Also share infrastructure readiness indicators, including:

- Immutable backup coverage
- Segmentation of high-value systems
- Incident playbook updates and usage in drills
- Endpoint detection and response (EDR) effectiveness scores

For executive engagement, summarize ransomware scenarios tested:

"In March, we simulated a ransomware attack targeting our Radiology PACS. Recovery time exceeded expectations by 27%, prompting a refresh of our downtime protocol and vendor SLAs."

Use these briefings to secure support for investments in:

- Backup infrastructure
- Endpoint security platforms
- Email filtering and phishing simulation tools
- Disaster recovery and cloud failover capabilities

Frame your reports to show how ransomware resilience is an **enterprise-wide initiative**, not just an IT function.

---

5. Report Audit Results and CAPA (Corrective and Preventive Actions)

Leadership needs visibility into **compliance health and audit performance**, including the hospital's ability to detect, correct, and prevent security gaps. As CISO, you should deliver regular updates on:

- Internal HIPAA audit results
- Policy compliance scores by department
- Third-party assessment outcomes (e.g., penetration tests, risk assessments)
- Number of findings or observations and their severity

Summarize CAPA efforts using a **risk-action-status matrix**, including:

- Identified risk or control gap
- Assigned department or owner
- Due date for resolution
- Completion status (Not Started, In Progress, Closed)
- Residual risk after remediation

Include timelines and milestones, and highlight:

- Risks that have lingered beyond their due date
- Mitigations completed under budget or ahead of schedule
- Projects needing board or C-suite sponsorship to complete

Translate these reports into operational terms:

"Our remote access audit found a 17% rate of inactive contractor accounts. This gap was closed with an IAM process update and monthly HR sync."

Consistent, transparent reporting of audit outcomes shows accountability, builds trust with leadership, and demonstrates the hospital's **commitment to continuous improvement** in compliance and risk governance.

6. Justify Cybersecurity Budget Tied to Hospital Risk Posture

Budget discussions with executive leadership and board members are a critical responsibility for every CISO. However, the ability to **secure appropriate funding** depends not on technical detail but on your ability to **connect cybersecurity investments directly to organizational risk and strategic priorities**.

Hospital leadership often views cybersecurity as a cost center until it's shown to directly impact patient safety, compliance, or continuity of operations. To justify your cybersecurity budget:

- Begin by **mapping requests to the hospital's risk register**, showing how each proposed investment addresses a specific, documented risk.
- Align spending proposals with **regulatory requirements** (HIPAA, OCR guidance, Joint Commission readiness).
- Link budget requests to past incidents or gaps highlighted in internal audits or vendor assessments.

Structure your presentation to leadership around these core elements:

1. **Current risk landscape**: Summarize emerging threats affecting the healthcare sector (e.g., ransomware, third-party breaches, phishing).
2. **Unaddressed risks**: List known gaps in controls, tools, or training that cannot be mitigated without funding.
3. **Proposed investments**: Itemize tools, services, or personnel needs, providing:
   - Cost estimates (CAPEX/OPEX)
   - Risk(s) addressed
   - Expected ROI (e.g., reduction in breach likelihood or cost of response)
4. **Impact on operations**: Explain how the investment supports uptime, patient care, and compliance efforts.
5. **Cost of inaction**: Model potential losses using breach cost data (e.g., average cost of a healthcare data breach per record).

Example justification:

"Investing $300K in a new Privileged Access Management solution will mitigate our top-ranked risk of unauthorized EHR access. Without it, a breach involving 10,000 records could result in $4.5M in OCR fines and class action exposure."

Additional tips for budget success:

- Include **benchmarks** from peer hospitals or frameworks like HIMSS, Ponemon, or H-ISAC.
- Tie requests to **strategic business initiatives**, such as expanding telehealth or migrating to hybrid cloud systems.
- Illustrate **progression and maturity** by comparing current year spending to previous years, highlighting improvement or underfunded areas.

Use **dashboards** and visual aids (pie charts, stacked bar graphs, roadmaps) to present complex budgets in an accessible format for non-technical audiences.

Finally, reinforce the idea that **cybersecurity is an enabler of hospital resilience**. With the right funding, the cybersecurity program doesn't just prevent breaches—it empowers the entire organization to deliver safe, uninterrupted patient care.

Chapter 6 Keywords and Definitions

- **Executive Dashboard**
  A visual reporting tool that summarizes cybersecurity metrics and risks in a format tailored for hospital leadership and board members. Often includes PHI breach data, HIPAA compliance status, and high-priority risks.
- **PHI Breach Risk**
  The probability and potential impact of unauthorized access, disclosure, or compromise of Protected Health Information. Must be continuously monitored and communicated to leadership.
- **HIPAA Compliance Metrics**
  Quantitative indicators used to measure the hospital's adherence to the HIPAA Privacy and Security Rules, including audit results, access control implementation, and incident response readiness.
- **Patient Safety Risk Translation**
  The practice of framing cyber threats in terms of how they may negatively affect clinical care, treatment delays, medical errors, or overall patient health outcomes.
- **Incident Scorecard**
  A standardized summary of a cybersecurity incident, including its severity, operational impact, containment status, and lessons learned. Used to communicate with executives and governance bodies.
- **Ransomware Readiness**
  The hospital's ability to prevent, detect, respond to, and recover from ransomware attacks. Includes technical controls, playbook testing, backup verification, and simulation exercises.
- **Drill Metrics**
  Quantitative results from cybersecurity simulation exercises (e.g., ransomware or phishing drills), such as response time, recovery time, and staff performance.
- **Corrective and Preventive Actions (CAPA)**
  Documented steps taken to remediate identified compliance gaps or security weaknesses, with assigned ownership, deadlines, and status tracking.

- **Risk-to-Budget Alignment**
  A strategy for justifying cybersecurity spending by linking each line item to a documented risk in the hospital's risk register or compliance roadmap.
- **Return on Security Investment (ROSI)**
  A measure of the effectiveness or value of a cybersecurity investment, typically framed as risk reduction, breach cost avoidance, or operational improvement.
- **Board Reporting**
  The structured communication process by which the CISO informs the hospital's board of directors or governance committees about the organization's cybersecurity posture and risk exposure.
- **Strategic Risk Communication**
  The act of conveying cybersecurity issues and decisions in a language aligned with organizational priorities such as patient care, compliance, and financial health.
- **Operational Impact Assessment**
  An analysis showing how a cyber incident or vulnerability could affect hospital workflows, staffing, and care delivery—used to emphasize the urgency of mitigation.
- **Mean Time to Detect (MTTD)**
  The average time it takes to identify a cybersecurity incident after it occurs, used as a performance metric for monitoring and detection capabilities.
- **Mean Time to Recover (MTTR)**
  The average duration required to restore full functionality after a cyber incident, used to measure incident response and business continuity performance.
- **Immutable Backups**
  Secure, unchangeable backup systems that cannot be altered or deleted by attackers. Essential for ransomware recovery and regulatory compliance.
- **Security Governance Maturity**
  The level of an organization's capability in managing cybersecurity risks, policies, and controls. Maturity is often measured through frameworks or audits.
- **Visual Risk Mapping**
  The use of charts or infographics (e.g., risk heat maps, care journey overlays) to communicate cyber risks and their business or clinical implications to non-technical stakeholders.
- **Budgetary Roadmap**
  A strategic plan outlining current and projected cybersecurity spending, typically presented with justifications, milestones, and risk mitigation goals.
- **Regulatory Breach Exposure**
  The financial, operational, and legal consequences of failing to meet breach notification or HIPAA security requirements. Often quantified in risk reports.

Chapter 7: Supervise Security Operations Center (SOC)

1. Monitor for EHR Anomalies, Privilege Escalations, and Lateral Movement

A hospital's **Electronic Health Record (EHR)** is among its most critical assets—and one of its most frequently targeted. CISOs must ensure that the Security Operations Center (SOC) continuously monitors for abnormal behavior across EHR platforms to detect early indicators of compromise, privilege misuse, or insider abuse.

Effective monitoring starts with a **baseline of normal behavior**:

- Typical login times and geolocations for physicians and nurses
- Expected data access volumes by role (e.g., nurses accessing 5–10 patient charts per hour)
- Common activity during shift changes, handoffs, or on-call rotations

The SOC must implement alerting for **privilege escalations** that deviate from norms, such as:

- A front desk staff member accessing administrative controls
- A nurse account suddenly gaining pharmacy-level access
- An IT account provisioning privileges without change control approval

Lateral movement detection—when an attacker jumps between systems to escalate control—is especially crucial in hospitals, where endpoint isolation is often weak due to shared workstations and minimal segmentation. SOC tools should monitor for:

- Multiple system logins by a single user in rapid succession
- Credential reuse across departments
- Attempts to access systems or files beyond a user's department

Use **User and Entity Behavior Analytics (UEBA)** to support these efforts. Tools that model behavior and detect deviations can significantly reduce false positives and focus analysts on meaningful threats.

Ensure that all alerts feed into a centralized **Security Information and Event Management (SIEM)** platform where they are correlated with logs, endpoint telemetry, and threat intelligence for comprehensive situational awareness.

2. Detect Unusual Data Flows from Imaging, Pharmacy, and Lab Systems

While much SOC activity focuses on traditional endpoints and network traffic, hospitals present unique challenges: data flows between **clinical systems** like imaging (PACS), pharmacy databases, and lab platforms (LIS). These systems are integral to patient care and often connected to third-party apps or cloud-based analytics services, making them potential attack vectors.

CISOs must ensure the SOC:

- Understands standard data workflows (e.g., lab-to-EHR results, prescription submission to pharmacy databases, imaging scans routed to specialists)
- Monitors for anomalies such as:
    - Unusually large file transfers from PACS systems
    - Non-standard protocols or ports in use during data transmission
    - Lab results being accessed at non-typical hours or in bulk
    - Outbound data flows to unapproved IP addresses or cloud platforms

SOC analysts must be equipped with **data flow diagrams** of these interconnected systems, created in partnership with Clinical Informatics, Radiology, and Pharmacy leaders.

If budget permits, hospitals should consider deploying **Data Loss Prevention (DLP)** and **Network Detection and Response (NDR)** tools with tailored rulesets for healthcare environments. These tools can alert when large volumes of PHI are in motion, when encrypted tunnels are established unexpectedly, or when data exfiltration behaviors are detected.

Finally, ensure logs from these systems are properly normalized and ingested into the SIEM to support historical analysis and alert correlation.

---

3. Correlate Logs from Medical Devices (Ventilators, Pumps) with Enterprise SIEM

Hospitals are increasingly reliant on **Internet of Medical Things (IoMT)** devices such as smart infusion pumps, ventilators, and patient monitors. These devices collect, transmit, and sometimes even modify patient care data—making them both operationally critical and cybersecurity targets.

The SOC must be able to **collect and correlate logs from medical devices** with enterprise data sources. Challenges include:

- Lack of standardized logging in many clinical devices
- Use of proprietary protocols

- Devices lacking onboard security telemetry

To address these, CISOs should work with **Biomedical Engineering and Clinical IT** to:

- Identify which devices can export logs (Syslog, SNMP, vendor APIs)
- Implement secure gateways or middleware to collect logs from legacy devices
- Ensure device logs are time-synchronized with the enterprise NTP servers
- Integrate logs into the SIEM for behavioral correlation

Once data is ingested, SOC analysts can correlate:

- Device access attempts with user badge data or login events
- Firmware updates with change control tickets
- Clinical alerts (e.g., alarms or thresholds exceeded) with network anomalies

This correlation enables early detection of threats like:

- Rogue commands issued to infusion pumps
- Unauthorized firmware changes on ventilators
- Malware attempting to exploit embedded systems

Documenting these correlations is essential for both **HIPAA security requirements** and future **FDA postmarket guidance compliance**.

4. Define Thresholds for Alerting on Hospital-Specific Indicators of Compromise

Every healthcare environment is unique, and so too are its threats. A proactive SOC must operate with a finely tuned set of **hospital-specific indicators of compromise (IOCs)—** custom rules that reflect real risks in your clinical, administrative, and infrastructure systems.

The CISO should guide the SOC in defining and refining alert thresholds for events such as:

- More than X PHI records accessed in Y minutes
- Failed login attempts across multiple clinical systems in a short span
- Access to high-profile patient charts by unauthorized roles
- Use of forbidden software on clinical workstations (e.g., P2P, screen-sharing tools)
- Outbound traffic to known malicious IPs from imaging or lab networks

The thresholds should be:

- Tuned to department workflows (e.g., high-access departments like ER may have higher limits)
- Reviewed monthly to reduce false positives and adapt to operational changes
- Developed in collaboration with clinical leads to understand acceptable variance

Use threat intelligence sources like **H-ISAC**, **MITRE ATT&CK**, and internal red team exercises to build and test custom IOCs.

Automated alerting should trigger:

- SOC response and triage tickets
- Notifications to clinical or IT leadership (depending on context)
- Activation of IR playbooks if thresholds indicate active compromise

Regular **threshold audits** ensure alerts remain relevant, actionable, and optimized for hospital-specific risk scenarios.

5. Conduct Forensic Reviews of Endpoint Incidents on Shared Nursing Stations

Hospital environments often use **shared workstations** at nursing stations, in patient rooms, and on mobile carts (Workstations on Wheels—WOWs). These endpoints are high-risk due to:

- Frequent logins/logouts
- Limited physical security
- High exposure to clinical software and PHI

When suspicious activity occurs on shared devices—malware infection, unauthorized software installation, or inappropriate access—SOC teams must conduct rapid and thorough **forensic reviews** to determine cause, scope, and impact.

Forensic reviews should include:

- Collection and analysis of endpoint logs (e.g., process creation, file access)
- Timeline reconstruction of user sessions (based on badge access, login/logout records)
- Correlation with network telemetry (e.g., data exfiltration attempts)
- Review of user keystrokes or screenshots if EDR tooling supports it
- Verification of patient data viewed or altered during the session

Collaborate with IT and nursing leadership to:

- Isolate affected devices and reimage as needed

- Interview staff involved for context or insight
- Document incident findings for compliance reporting

Ensure that **SOC analysts are trained in healthcare-specific forensic techniques**, including how to handle protected data, preserve chain of custody, and communicate findings with sensitivity to clinical stakeholders.

6. Ensure SOC Analysts Receive Healthcare-Specific Training

A well-equipped Security Operations Center (SOC) relies not only on advanced tools but on highly trained analysts who understand the unique nature of the **healthcare environment**. Unlike corporate SOCs, hospital SOC teams must interpret alerts through the lens of **clinical workflows, regulatory mandates, patient safety concerns, and specialized technologies** like IoMT devices and EHR systems.

To maintain an effective SOC, the CISO must ensure that analysts receive **ongoing, role-specific training** tailored to healthcare security.

Training Curriculum Essentials:

- **HIPAA Security and Privacy Rules**: Analysts must understand what constitutes PHI, how it should be handled, and the breach notification obligations tied to security incidents.
- **Clinical System Familiarity**: Training should include overviews of systems like EHR (Epic, Cerner), PACS, LIS, and pharmacy systems. Analysts should be able to recognize typical vs. anomalous behavior within these platforms.
- **Healthcare Workflow Awareness**: Staff must understand clinical routines—such as how nurses share carts or how physicians access systems during rounds—so they can differentiate between legitimate activity and threat indicators.
- **Medical Device Security (IoMT)**: SOC analysts should be familiar with common medical devices, their operating systems, communication protocols, and known vulnerabilities. Integration with biomedical teams is essential.

Tools and Platforms:

- **SIEM Training**: Ensure analysts are proficient in the hospital's SIEM tools (e.g., Splunk, IBM QRadar, LogRhythm) and understand how to query logs from healthcare-specific systems.
- **EDR and NDR Solutions**: Analysts should be fluent in managing endpoint detection and network traffic anomaly tools deployed across both administrative and clinical zones.
- **Threat Intelligence Tools**: Training on interpreting IOCs and threat data from H-ISAC, MITRE ATT&CK for Healthcare, and proprietary sources is essential for proactive defense.

Role-Specific Skills:

- **Tier 1 Analysts**: Focus on triage, ticketing, and initial alert validation—must understand when and how to escalate alerts related to patient data.
- **Tier 2/3 Analysts**: Deeper training in forensic analysis, incident response workflows, and communication with legal/compliance teams.
- **SOC Leadership**: Training in healthcare regulations, executive communication, and coordination with risk management and emergency preparedness leaders.

Training Delivery Methods:

- **Onboarding bootcamps** for new analysts tailored to hospital operations
- **Monthly knowledge sharing sessions** covering real-world incidents, internal cases, or external breaches
- **Simulation exercises** such as red team/blue team drills, EHR breach scenarios, and device exploitation walkthroughs
- **External certifications** such as:
  o HCISPP (Healthcare Certified Information Security and Privacy Practitioner)
  o CHPS (Certified in Healthcare Privacy and Security)
  o CEH, CISSP with healthcare-specific modules or electives

Collaboration and Immersion:

In addition to formal instruction, encourage **cross-training with clinical teams**. Embedding SOC analysts temporarily in a nursing unit or allowing them to shadow clinicians helps them contextualize alerts and understand real-world risk implications.

Finally, incorporate **metrics** into your training program to track analyst growth:

- Reduction in false positive rates
- Time to escalation for PHI-related alerts
- Successful detection of simulated insider threats
- Improved communication in IR exercises

By investing in specialized training, the CISO ensures the SOC is not just a reactive function—but a **strategic security partner embedded within the hospital's mission to deliver safe, uninterrupted care.**

Chapter 7 Keywords and Definitions

- **Security Operations Center (SOC)**
  A centralized team and facility responsible for monitoring, detecting, analyzing, and responding to cybersecurity incidents in real-time. In a hospital, the SOC focuses on protecting clinical systems, PHI, and medical devices.
- **Electronic Health Record (EHR) Monitoring**
  The continuous observation of EHR access and activity logs to detect anomalies

such as unauthorized access, data manipulation, and usage outside of clinical scope.

- **Privilege Escalation Detection**
  The identification of unauthorized increases in user access levels, such as a nurse gaining administrator rights or a clerk accessing prescribing functions.
- **Lateral Movement**
  A technique used by attackers to spread across systems within a network after initial access. Detection in hospitals is critical to prevent widespread compromise across departments and clinical zones.
- **User and Entity Behavior Analytics (UEBA)**
  Security technology that uses machine learning to establish normal behavior patterns for users and devices, then alerts on deviations that may indicate compromise or insider threats.
- **Clinical System Anomaly Detection**
  The practice of monitoring systems like PACS, LIS, and pharmacy tools for abnormal data flows or access patterns, indicating potential exfiltration, misconfiguration, or attack.
- **Data Loss Prevention (DLP)**
  A security strategy and toolset designed to monitor, detect, and prevent the unauthorized transmission of sensitive data such as PHI outside the hospital network.
- **Network Detection and Response (NDR)**
  A cybersecurity solution that analyzes network traffic to identify suspicious behavior, such as unusual communication patterns or data transfers in clinical systems.
- **Internet of Medical Things (IoMT)**
  Connected medical devices that collect, transmit, or process patient data. These devices require special monitoring due to their unique protocols and clinical relevance.
- **Security Information and Event Management (SIEM)**
  A centralized platform used to collect, analyze, and correlate logs and security data from across hospital systems, enabling real-time alerting and historical analysis.
- **Indicators of Compromise (IOCs)**
  Data points such as file hashes, IP addresses, or behavior patterns that indicate a potential or confirmed security breach. Hospitals often develop custom IOCs based on their environment.
- **Hospital-Specific Alert Thresholds**
  Customized alert settings based on normal clinical activity and risk tolerance. These thresholds help reduce false positives and ensure alerts are relevant to hospital workflows.
- **Endpoint Forensics**
  The process of collecting and analyzing data from hospital devices (e.g., WOWs, nursing station PCs) to determine the source and scope of a cyber incident.
- **Workstations on Wheels (WOWs)**
  Mobile computing stations used by clinical staff for bedside care. Due to their

shared nature, they are high-risk endpoints requiring focused forensic and access review.

- **Shared Device Risk Management**
  The application of special monitoring and forensic strategies to devices used by multiple staff members, where attribution and control are more complex.
- **Healthcare-Specific SOC Training**
  Training programs tailored for SOC analysts in hospital environments, covering HIPAA, clinical workflows, medical device security, and PHI protection.
- **Clinical Workflow Contextualization**
  Understanding how clinical routines impact system access, which helps SOC analysts distinguish legitimate user behavior from suspicious activity.
- **Medical Device Logging Integration**
  The process of capturing and correlating logs from ventilators, pumps, and monitors into enterprise SOC tools for better threat detection.
- **Forensic Chain of Custody**
  A documented process to preserve digital evidence from collection to analysis, ensuring integrity for compliance investigations or legal proceedings.
- **Red Team/Blue Team Simulation**
  Cybersecurity exercises where a simulated attacker (red team) tests the defenses of a responder group (blue team), often used in SOC training to improve detection and response capabilities.

Appendix A: Keywords and Definitions

Access Control Policy
A documented set of rules governing who can access what data, under which conditions, and through what means.

Audit Trail
A recorded history of access and activity across systems, used for forensic investigation, regulatory compliance, and policy enforcement.

Behavioral Analytics (UEBA)
User and Entity Behavior Analytics is a technique that uses machine learning to identify deviations from normal patterns in user behavior, helping detect insider threats and compromised accounts.

Board Reporting
The structured communication process by which the CISO informs hospital leadership or the board of directors about cybersecurity posture, risks, and compliance standing.

Bring Your Own Device (BYOD)
A policy that governs how personal devices can be securely used by employees to access hospital systems, typically with controls such as MDM, encryption, and usage monitoring.

Code Cyber
A hospital-specific escalation system that categorizes the severity of a cybersecurity incident and triggers predefined response procedures across clinical and administrative environments.

Compliance Liaison Program
A decentralized model where each hospital department designates a point-of-contact responsible for promoting cybersecurity awareness, enforcing policy, and coordinating with the CISO.

Corrective Action Plan (CAP)
A documented response to an audit finding or incident, outlining steps to remediate deficiencies, prevent recurrence, and monitor progress.

Cybersecurity Governance
The structured framework of policies, procedures, and controls that guide the management of cybersecurity risk across the hospital enterprise.

Data Protection
Measures taken to ensure the confidentiality, integrity, and availability of patient and hospital data against unauthorized access, disclosure, or destruction.

Downtime Protocols
Predefined procedures that guide clinical and administrative staff in continuing safe patient care during IT outages or system failures, such as EHR downtime or ransomware events.

Electronic Health Records (EHR)
Digital systems used to collect, store, and manage patient health data. EHRs are central to healthcare operations and a primary target for cyber threats.

Emergency Access Procedures (Break-Glass Access)
Special access privileges granted to authorized personnel during clinical emergencies, allowing overrides of standard access controls, with audit logging for accountability.

Endpoint Forensics
The process of collecting and analyzing data from hospital endpoints (e.g., shared nursing stations, WOWs) to determine the source, scope, and impact of a cybersecurity incident.

FAIR Model
Factor Analysis of Information Risk is a quantitative risk analysis framework used to assess and compare cybersecurity risks in financial terms.

HITRUST CSF
A certifiable security and privacy framework that incorporates healthcare-specific regulations like HIPAA, mapping them to multiple industry standards (NIST, ISO, etc.).

HIPAA Compliance
Adherence to the Health Insurance Portability and Accountability Act's security and privacy rules for safeguarding PHI through administrative, technical, and physical safeguards.

Incident Response (IR) Playbook
A detailed guide outlining procedures to detect, respond to, and recover from cybersecurity incidents, tailored to hospital systems and threats.

Incident Scorecard
A standardized summary of a cybersecurity incident used to inform executives and governance committees, including impact, recovery status, and lessons learned.

Internal Audit Coordination
Collaboration between the cybersecurity team and hospital internal audit department to evaluate and document cyber risk, policy adherence, and remediation progress.

Joint Commission Standards
Regulatory guidelines established by The Joint Commission, which include cybersecurity components tied to healthcare quality and patient safety accreditation.

Mobile Device Management (MDM)
Technology that enforces security policies on mobile devices used to access hospital systems, including encryption, remote wipe, and app control.

Multifactor Authentication (MFA)
A security mechanism requiring two or more verification methods—such as passwords and biometrics—to gain access to sensitive hospital systems.

Patient Safety
The avoidance of unintended or unexpected harm to patients during healthcare delivery, supported by secure and reliable information systems.

PHI Breach Risk
The probability and potential impact of unauthorized access, disclosure, or compromise of Protected Health Information within the hospital's digital environment.

Post-Incident Review (PIR)
A formal evaluation conducted after a cybersecurity incident or drill to assess response performance and update plans based on lessons learned.

Protected Health Information (PHI)
Any information that can identify an individual and relates to their past, present, or future physical or mental health or healthcare services. Protected under HIPAA.

Ransomware Readiness
The hospital's ability to prevent, detect, respond to, and recover from ransomware attacks, measured through technical controls and response testing.

Return on Security Investment (ROSI)
A calculation or justification that evaluates the value or effectiveness of cybersecurity spending in terms of risk reduction or cost avoidance.

Risk Assessment
A structured process used to identify, evaluate, and prioritize cybersecurity risks based on likelihood, impact, and control effectiveness.

Risk Register
A centralized document or platform used to track known cyber risks, their severity, mitigation actions, owners, and current status.

Role-Based Access Control (RBAC)
An access control method in which users are granted permissions based on their job role or department within the hospital.

Security Information and Event Management (SIEM)
A platform that collects, analyzes, and correlates security event data from various hospital systems to support threat detection and incident response.

Third-Party Risk Management
The practice of assessing and monitoring the security practices of vendors, business associates, and contractors who access hospital systems or data.

User and Entity Behavior Analytics (UEBA)
Technology that monitors baseline behaviors of users and devices to detect abnormal activities that may indicate threats or compromised accounts.

Zero Trust Architecture (ZTA)
A security model that assumes no user or device is inherently trusted and enforces strict identity verification and access controls at all times.

Appendix B: CISO Task Checklist

Use this checklist as a strategic roadmap for managing and validating your cybersecurity leadership activities in a hospital setting.

Chapter 1: Develop and Maintain the Healthcare Cybersecurity Strategy

☐ Align cybersecurity priorities with patient safety and clinical outcomes

☐ Map strategy to HIPAA, HITECH, and Joint Commission standards

☐ Conduct comprehensive, department-specific risk assessments

☐ Include ransomware response planning in strategic initiatives

☐ Coordinate with clinical leadership on cybersecurity alignment

☐ Update strategy based on H-ISAC threat intelligence

☐ Define Zero Trust and endpoint resilience milestones

Chapter 2: Establish Governance and Security Policies

☐ Maintain hospital-wide HIPAA-aligned security policies

☐ Define policies for EMR access, BYOD, and remote use

☐ Create emergency access procedures (break-glass controls)

☐ Establish IoMT device access and usage guidelines

☐ Appoint departmental compliance liaisons

☐ Include stakeholders in policy creation and review

Chapter 3: Oversee Risk Management and Assessment Programs

☐ Perform annual HIPAA Security Rule risk assessments

☐ Maintain and update a PHI-focused risk register

☐ Evaluate risks tied to care interruptions and medical devices

☐ Use frameworks (NIST, HITRUST, FAIR) for risk analysis

☐ Prioritize and report risks based on clinical and operational impact

☐ Track remediation through dashboards and executive summaries

☐ Integrate cybersecurity into project/change management

☐ Assess third-party/vendor risks and contract exposure

☐ Conduct tabletop and scenario-based risk exercises

☐ Prepare board-level risk and mitigation reports

Chapter 4: Lead Incident Response Planning and Execution

☐ Maintain a current IR playbook tailored to hospital workflows

☐ Define Code Cyber response levels and triggers

☐ Develop downtime protocols with clinical departments

☐ Test EHR recovery quarterly through full simulations

☐ Conduct phishing-based breach simulations regularly

☐ Involve legal, compliance, and privacy teams in breach workflows

☐ Integrate cyber incidents into hospital emergency plans

☐ Establish off-band communication plans for cyber emergencies

☐ Preserve digital evidence through proper forensic practices

☐ Hold post-incident reviews and update response plans accordingly

Chapter 5: Conduct Regular Security Audits and Compliance Reviews

☐ Perform internal HIPAA audits and policy compliance checks

☐ Review user access logs for PHI misuse or snooping

☐ Audit contractor and student remote access

☐ Validate system logging for EHR, PACS, and LIS

☐ Align with CMS, OCR, and Joint Commission audit frameworks

☐ Coordinate with internal and third-party audit teams

☐ Track CAPA implementation with deadlines and owners

Chapter 6: Report to Executive Leadership and Hospital Board

☐ Deliver visual dashboards on PHI risk and HIPAA compliance

☐ Translate cyber threats into clinical impact scenarios

☐ Provide executive briefings on incident impact and response

☐ Share ransomware preparedness metrics and drill outcomes

☐ Report audit findings and CAPA status

☐ Justify cybersecurity budget with risk alignment and ROI

Chapter 7: Supervise Security Operations Center (SOC)

☐ Monitor EHR for privilege escalation and lateral movement

☐ Detect abnormal data flows from lab, imaging, and pharmacy systems

☐ Correlate IoMT logs with enterprise SIEM data

☐ Customize alert thresholds for hospital-specific IOCs

☐ Conduct endpoint forensics on shared clinical workstations

☐ Provide continuous

Appendix C: Sample Incident Response Playbook Templates

Incident Response Lifecycle Overview (NIST Model)

1. Preparation

- Maintain updated contact lists (IT, legal, privacy, clinical leads)

- Define IR team roles and responsibilities

- Train staff on reporting procedures and "Code Cyber" levels

- Maintain and test backup systems and downtime protocols

- Store printed IR playbooks and communication flowcharts

2. Detection and Analysis

- Use SIEM to correlate unusual access or network activity

- Define hospital-specific indicators of compromise (IOCs)

- Verify alerts involving PHI access, credential misuse, or ransomware

- Document detection source, scope, and timeline

- Initiate Code Cyber alert (Green/Yellow/Red)

3. Containment, Eradication, and Recovery

- Short-term containment: isolate affected systems or devices

- Long-term containment: change passwords, restrict access

- Eradicate malware or malicious users

- Recover from clean backups or failover systems

- Validate system integrity before restoring operations

- Notify legal/privacy officers to begin breach impact analysis

4. Post-Incident Activity

- Conduct Post-Incident Review (PIR)

- Document timeline, actions taken, lessons learned

- Update playbook, policies, and training based on findings

- Submit breach reports (if PHI was compromised) within HIPAA's 60-day window

- Prepare board-level summary of incident response effectiveness

Incident Severity Classification (Code Cyber Levels)

Code Cyber - Green: Low severity (e.g., phishing email blocked, minor malware flagged). Action: SOC triage and log review.

Code Cyber - Yellow: Moderate severity (e.g., unauthorized access to multiple records, failed login attempts). Action: IR Team activation, stakeholder notifications.

Code Cyber - Red: High severity (e.g., ransomware attack, PHI exfiltration, major system outage). Action: Full IR response, CISO-led coordination, regulatory engagement.

PHI Breach Notification Checklist

- ☐ Complete a risk assessment (type, extent, and recipient of PHI)
- ☐ Involve legal and privacy teams immediately
- ☐ Determine if notification is required under HIPAA
- ☐ Notify affected individuals within 60 days
- ☐ Notify OCR and, if >500 records, local media
- ☐ Coordinate with PR on patient communication
- ☐ Preserve logs and evidence (chain of custody)

Sample Incident Reporting Form

Date/Time Detected:

System(s) Affected:

Detection Source (SIEM/Helpdesk/etc.):

Incident Type: (Phishing / Malware / Unauthorized Access / Ransomware / Other)

PHI Exposure Involved? ☐ Yes ☐ No

Initial Containment Action:

IR Team Members Engaged:

Next Steps & Follow-up:

Key Templates to Maintain (Editable)

- Incident Response Flowchart (who does what and when)

- Communication Escalation Matrix (who gets informed and how)

- Code Cyber Activation Guide (when to escalate)

- Notification Letter Templates (for patients, OCR, partners)

- Internal Executive Brief Template (post-incident report)

Appendix D: Templates for Incident Response

These templates serve as essential, ready-to-customize tools for streamlining hospital cybersecurity incident response. Each one is designed for practical use in coordination with IR teams, compliance officers, clinical stakeholders, and hospital leadership.

1. Incident Response Flowchart (Roles and Responsibilities)

Purpose:
Visualize who does what during a cybersecurity event—ideal for wall posters, IR binders, and executive briefings.

Key Elements to Include:

- Flow of communication from detection to resolution
- Specific responsibilities for IT Security, Legal, Privacy, and Clinical Ops
- Trigger points for each phase of the IR lifecycle
- Incident Commander designation
- Contacts for vendor coordination and escalation

Tip:
Use swimlanes to show department roles side-by-side during each stage (Detection, Containment, Recovery).

2. Communication Escalation Matrix

Purpose:
Ensures the right people are notified at the right time, reducing confusion and speeding up response.

Template Sections:

- Code Cyber level (Green / Yellow / Red)
- Who to notify (CIO, CMO, Compliance Officer, Legal, PR, etc.)
- Communication method (Email, Phone, Pager, Secure Messaging App)
- Required response time (e.g., "Notify within 30 minutes of classification")

Tip:
Include internal and external contacts, and mark off-hours or weekend alternates.

3. Code Cyber Activation Guide

Purpose:
Defines when and how to escalate a cybersecurity incident using the "Code Cyber" system.

Template Content:

- Severity criteria for Green, Yellow, and Red levels
- Examples (e.g., PHI snooping = Yellow; ransomware in EHR = Red)
- Response team members involved per level
- Hospital-wide broadcast or silent alert process
- Who authorizes escalation (typically the CISO or on-call lead)

Tip:
Preload into your paging system or incident management app for one-click activation.

---

4. Notification Letter Templates

Purpose:
Saves time and ensures legal consistency when notifying patients, partners, or regulators after a PHI breach.

Types of Letters to Include:

- Patient breach notification
- OCR breach notification
- Business associate incident notice
- State AG notification (if required)
- Media/public disclosure (for breaches affecting 500+ patients)

Tip:
Draft in plain language and pre-fill static fields (e.g., hospital name, contact info). Include checkboxes for personalization fields like name, date of service, and what was compromised.

---

5. Internal Executive Brief Template

Purpose:
Quickly communicate the incident's impact, response status, and next steps to the executive team and hospital board.

Key Fields to Include:

- Date/Time of Incident
- Detection Source
- Affected Systems and Scope
- PHI Involved (Yes/No + Summary)
- Downtime or Clinical Impact
- Containment and Recovery Actions
- Legal/Compliance Actions
- Outstanding Risks
- Lessons Learned and Recommendations

Tip:
Use bullet points and keep it under 1 page for C-Suite clarity. Include a RYG visual indicator for severity and risk trend.

Appendix E: Third-Party Risk Assessment Questionnaire

This questionnaire helps assess whether vendors and business associates meet the hospital's cybersecurity standards, HIPAA requirements, and operational risk thresholds. It can be used during vendor onboarding, annual reviews, or prior to contract renewals.

Section 1: General Information

- Organization Name:
- Primary Contact Name and Title:
- Email Address / Phone Number:
- Services Provided to the Hospital:
- Will the vendor access, store, process, or transmit PHI? ☐ Yes ☐ No
- Is there a signed Business Associate Agreement (BAA)? ☐ Yes ☐ No

---

Section 2: Regulatory and Legal Compliance

1. Is your organization subject to HIPAA or HITECH compliance? ☐ Yes ☐ No
2. Are you compliant with any of the following frameworks? (Check all that apply)
   ☐ HIPAA ☐ HITRUST ☐ NIST CSF ☐ ISO/IEC 27001 ☐ SOC 2 ☐ GDPR
3. Do you conduct regular internal or external compliance audits? ☐ Yes ☐ No
4. Do you have an incident response plan that includes breach notification timelines? ☐ Yes ☐ No
5. Are you prepared to notify the hospital within 24 hours of a data breach? ☐ Yes ☐ No

---

Section 3: Technical Security Controls

1. Do you use multi-factor authentication (MFA) for all remote access? ☐ Yes ☐ No
2. Are all systems and data encrypted in transit and at rest? ☐ Yes ☐ No
3. Are all employee devices (laptops, mobile, etc.) managed under an MDM solution? ☐ Yes ☐ No
4. Do you conduct regular vulnerability scans and penetration tests? ☐ Yes ☐ No
5. Are software and operating system patches applied within 30 days? ☐ Yes ☐ No

6. Do you monitor user access logs and anomalous behavior? ☐ Yes ☐ No

---

Section 4: Personnel and Access Management

1. Do all employees with system access undergo background checks? ☐ Yes ☐ No
2. Are employees trained on HIPAA and cybersecurity awareness annually? ☐ Yes ☐ No
3. Is access to hospital data based on least privilege and role-based controls? ☐ Yes ☐ No
4. Is user access reviewed and updated quarterly or upon role changes? ☐ Yes ☐ No
5. Are accounts of former employees disabled within 24 hours of departure? ☐ Yes ☐ No

---

Section 5: Cloud Services and Data Hosting

1. Do you host hospital data in the cloud? ☐ Yes ☐ No
   o If yes, specify the cloud provider: _____
2. Is your cloud infrastructure covered under a shared responsibility model? ☐ Yes ☐ No
3. Do you have visibility and control over all data access points in the cloud? ☐ Yes ☐ No
4. Are cloud configurations regularly audited for misconfigurations? ☐ Yes ☐ No

---

Section 6: Incident Management and Business Continuity

1. Do you have a documented business continuity and disaster recovery plan? ☐ Yes ☐ No
2. Have you tested your disaster recovery plan within the past 12 months? ☐ Yes ☐ No
3. Can you restore critical systems and data within agreed RTOs and RPOs? ☐ Yes ☐ No
4. Do you maintain logs of all security-related incidents and responses? ☐ Yes ☐ No
5. Do you provide incident summaries or root cause reports upon request? ☐ Yes ☐ No

Section 7: Subcontractors and Third Parties

1. Do you use subcontractors that may access hospital systems or data? ☐ Yes ☐ No
2. Do you assess your subcontractors for security and HIPAA compliance? ☐ Yes ☐ No
3. Are all subcontractors required to sign flow-down BAA agreements? ☐ Yes ☐ No
4. Are subcontractor activities monitored and audited? ☐ Yes ☐ No

Section 8: Certifications and Documentation (Attach Where Applicable)

1. Most recent SOC 2 Type II report
2. ISO 27001 Certification
3. HITRUST Certification Letter
4. HIPAA Risk Assessment Summary
5. Cyber Liability Insurance Certificate
6. Recent Penetration Test Summary

Appendix I: Audit-Ready Policy and Log Retention Matrix

This matrix provides a comprehensive reference for hospitals to ensure required cybersecurity and compliance records are retained appropriately. It aligns with regulatory expectations and audit preparedness.

Retention Matrix Structure

Document / Log Type	Description	Retention Period	Owner / Responsible Party	Applicable Regulation

1. Policies and Procedures

- **Information Security Policy**
  Overview of security controls, objectives, and roles.
  Retain: **6 years**
  Owner: CISO
  Regulation: HIPAA §164.316(b)(2)
- **Access Control Policy**
  Defines RBAC, least privilege, and access provisioning standards.
  Retain: **6 years**
  Owner: Identity & Access Manager
  Regulation: HIPAA, NIST SP 800-53
- **Incident Response Policy and Plan**
  Procedures for detecting, responding to, and recovering from incidents.
  Retain: **6 years** from last revision
  Owner: CISO / IR Lead
  Regulation: HIPAA, NIST CSF
- **Acceptable Use Policy**
  Guidelines for employee use of hospital IT resources.
  Retain: **6 years**
  Owner: HR / IT Security
  Regulation: HIPAA, HR Compliance

---

2. Logs and Audit Trails

- **System Access Logs (EHR, PACS, etc.)**
  Records of who accessed what data and when.
  Retain: **6 years**

Owner: IT Security / App Admin
Regulation: HIPAA §164.312(b)

- **Security Event Logs (SIEM)**
  Data on system events, anomalies, alerts, etc.
  Retain: **1–3 years** (based on risk policy)
  Owner: SOC Lead
  Regulation: NIST SP 800-92
- **Authentication Logs**
  Logs of user login, logout, and failed attempts.
  Retain: **1 year minimum**
  Owner: System Admin
  Regulation: HIPAA, NIST
- **Firewall / IDS / IPS Logs**
  Records of network-level traffic and threats.
  Retain: **1–2 years**
  Owner: Network Security Team
  Regulation: NIST SP 800-137
- **Email Gateway Logs**
  Includes spam, phishing, malware attempts.
  Retain: **1–2 years**
  Owner: Messaging Administrator
  Regulation: Organizational Risk Management

3. Audit and Risk Records

- **HIPAA Security Risk Assessment**
  Annual evaluation of controls, risks, and safeguards.
  Retain: **6 years**
  Owner: CISO / Compliance Officer
  Regulation: HIPAA §164.308(a)(1)(ii)(A)
- **Internal Audit Reports**
  Evidence of policy, control, or procedural evaluations.
  Retain: **7 years**
  Owner: Internal Audit
  Regulation: HIPAA, TJC, CMS
- **Third-Party Security Assessments**
  Vendor risk evaluations, SOC reports, penetration tests.
  Retain: **3–6 years**
  Owner: Vendor Risk Manager
  Regulation: HIPAA, Contractual

4. Training and Awareness

- **Security Awareness Training Records**
  Documentation of who completed what training, when.
  Retain: **6 years**
  Owner: HR / Compliance
  Regulation: HIPAA §164.308(a)(5)(i)
- **Phishing Simulation Results**
  Records of simulated attacks, user actions, and follow-ups.
  Retain: **2 years**
  Owner: Security Awareness Team
  Regulation: Organizational Policy

---

5. Incident and Breach Documentation

- **Incident Reports and Root Cause Analyses**
  Records of IR activities and lessons learned.
  Retain: **6 years**
  Owner: CISO / IR Lead
  Regulation: HIPAA Breach Rule, OCR
- **Breach Notification Documentation**
  Notifications to individuals, OCR, and media (if applicable).
  Retain: **6 years**
  Owner: Legal / Privacy Officer
  Regulation: HIPAA §164.404–408
- **Forensic Reports and Chain of Custody Logs**
  Digital evidence preservation from security events.
  Retain: **6+ years (legal holds apply)**
  Owner: IR Team / Legal
  Regulation: HIPAA, E-Discovery Rules